Promotion of Direct Investment in Developing Countries

mit Beiträgen von

F. Javier Alejo
Max Amstutz
C. Fred Bergsten
Hans-Martin Burkhardt
Heinz Hauser
Adolfo Hegewisch
Klaus Huber
Helmut Maucher
Hans Mayrzedt
Julian G. Y. Radcliffe
Hans Pollan
Ibrahim F. I. Shihata
Cornelio Sommaruga
Jörg-Dietrich Wurmstich

Verlag Rüegger

This volume is simultaneously published as Nr. I/86
of the quarterly «Aussenwirtschaft»
(The Swiss Review of International Economic Relations)

ISBN 3 7253 0268 5

INHALT

Industrie- und Entwicklungsländer sowie Vertreter der Weltbankgruppe sind sich weitgehend einig, dass Direktinvestitionen eine grössere Rolle bei der Finanzierung von Entwicklungsbedürfnissen spielen könnten und sollten; insbesondere da man nicht mit einer wesentlich höheren Neukreditvergabe der Banken rechnen kann, solange der Überhang an unfreiwillig gehaltenen Krediten nicht abgebaut ist. Da sich Unternehmen mit Direktinvestitionen langfristig binden, sind Stabilität und Glaubwürdigkeit der Investitionsordnungen der Empfängerländer von grösster Bedeutung für das Investitionsklima. Dieses Aktivum kann jedoch nur längerfristig aufgebaut werden, indem der Spielraum für künftige Politikveränderungen auf konstitutionaler Ebene eingeengt wird. Internationale Investitionsschutz-Abkommen und andere Institutionen zum Schutz vor Verlusten bei Direktinvestitionen – dazu gehört vor allem auch das neueste Projekt der Weltbank (MIGA) – können als internationale Verpflichtungen angesehen werden, die eine solche Verfassungsfunktion haben. Ebenso sollte die Allokationsfunktion des Marktes bei Risikokapitalflüssen so wenig wie möglich beeinträchtigt werden. Eine Einstellung, die auch der International Finance Corporation (IFC) als Basis für ihre Politik dient.

Obwohl die (stark ideologisch motivierte) Kontroverse um Nutzen und Schädlichkeit von ausländischen Direktinvestitionen in Entwicklungsländern an Bedeutung verloren hat, sind noch einige Probleme bei dieser Art des Kapitaltransfers zu lösen. Diese erscheinen aber insbesondere dann lösbar und zu einem gegenseitigen Nutzen zu führen, wenn beide Seiten – die Industrieländer (als Investitionsgeber) und die Entwicklungsländer (als Empfänger) – in den von ihnen beeinflussbaren Bereichen ernsthaft für verbesserte Voraussetzungen für einen erhöhten Fluss von Risikokapital sorgen.

Seite

Obwohl IFC in der Regel nur 10 bis 20% des gesamthaft benötigten Kapitals beisteuert, hat sie eine grosse Bedeutung für die Finanzierung einzelner Projekte. Dies zeigt ein Beispiel in Indien, wo sie eine Vergrösserung einer Fahrzeugfabrik mitfinanziert hat. IFC sucht aber auch nach neuen Wegen, wenn es gilt, Projekte zu ermöglichen, die speziell der Entwicklung einer Region dienen und unkonventionelle Massnahmen verlangen, wie beispielsweise bei einigen export-orientierten Betrieben in Jugoslawien. Ändern die wirtschaftlichen Bedingungen, wie etwa 1982 bei Ausbruch der lateinamerikanischen Schuldenkrise, versucht IFC auch durch eine rasche Anpassung an die geänderten Verhältnisse und der Suche nach neuen Massnahmen, die Anpassungskosten für die von ihr unterstützten Institutionen – gezeigt am Beispiel der BLADEX – zu senken.

IFC hat eine bedeutende Funktion beim Aufbrechen des Teufelskreises von mangelndem Vertrauen in die wirtschaftliche Situation vieler Entwicklungsländer und ungenügendem Kapitalfluss in diese Staaten. Durch die Übernahme eines gewissen Risikos, der Mitfinanzierung von Eigenkapital und einer flexiblen Haltung in schwierigen Zeiten gelingt es IFC, eine gute Basis für Investitionen privater Unternehmen in Entwicklungsländern zu schaffen. Durch eine relativ unbürokratische und privatsektor-orientierte Einstellung wird dieser positive Aspekt noch verstärkt, auch wenn der Entscheidungsprozess innerhalb der IFC noch beschleunigt werden sollte.

Für Geschäftsbanken werden Ko-Finanzierungen mit IFC oder anderen multilateralen Entwicklungsbanken eine immer wichtigere Methode, Entwicklungsländern Kapital für prioritäre Projekte zur Verfügung zu stellen. Entscheidend dafür ist, dass die von IFC geprüften Projekte von hoher Qualität sind und dass die «Schutzfunktion» von IFC bezüglich Erfüllung des Schuldendienstes gut funktioniert, dass also das Transfer-Risiko für die Banken stark gemindert wird. Trotz der bisher guten Zusammenarbeit bei Ko-Finanzierungen wird aber eine weitere Verbesserung bezüglich der Aufteilung der Risiken gewünscht, um damit die Voraussetzungen für eine zukünftige Erhöhung des Kapitalflusses zu schaffen. Neue Techniken müssen dafür geprüft und in die Tat umgesetzt werden wie etwa multilaterale Investitions-Garantien, etc.

Seite

Die besonderen Schwierigkeiten bei der Berechnung der politischen Risiken, denen längerfristige Investitionen im Ausland ausgesetzt sind, führten dazu, dass staatliche Institutionen als erste Versicherungsschutz dagegen anboten. Das Beispiel des Investitionsgarantie-Systems der Bundesrepublik Deutschland zeigt die breite Palette der Probleme in der Praxis, wenn Investitionen gegen Enteignungen, Kriegs- und Transferrisiken versichert werden sollen. Das vermehrte Auftreten von privaten Versicherungsgesellschaften in den letzten Jahren verlangt zudem nach Absprachen zwischen staatlichen und privaten Institutionen.

Private Institutionen bilden mehr eine Ergänzung zu den staatlichen Versicherungen gegen politische Risiken, als dass sie diese konkurrenzieren. Private können nämlich weder langfristig politische Risiken zu konstanten Prämien abdecken noch die gleichen Garantien bei Verlusten durch Kriege und bei Inkonvertibilität von Währungen geben. Hingegen zeichnen sie sich durch eine grosse Flexibilität aus, was sich positiv bei der Festlegung der Garantiesummen oder bei der Prämienberechnung niederschlägt. Zudem erbringen private Versicherer immer mehr Zusatzleistungen wie etwa die Beratung von Firmen in Fragen des politischen Risikomanagements und der Wiederbeschaffung von Verlusten, oder sie engagieren sich sogar in Verhandlungen mit den entsprechenden Stellen, wenn ein Schadensfall droht oder bereits eingetreten ist.

Aussenwirtschaft, 41. Jahrgang (1986), Heft I, Grüsch: Rüegger, S.9–18

Promotion of Foreign Direct Investment to Developing Countries: An Exercise in Cooperation

Prof. Dr. Heinz Hauser
University of St. Gallen

Renewed Interest in Foreign Direct Investment

The World Bank Group has taken several initiatives to promote foreign direct investment to developing countries. For example, credits for structural adjustments give special emphasis to programs directed at strengthening private investment in general. In 1985, the Board of Governors decided to double the working capital of the International Finance Corporation (IFC) — its affiliate organization specialized in promoting foreign direct investment to developing countries. Finally, at their annual meeting in Seoul in October 1985, the Governors adopted the Convention for the Creation of the Multilateral Investment Guarantee Agency (MIGA), which is open for ratification and will be established as an independent organization within the World Bank Group as soon as the minimal quorum requirement is met.

These initiatives are paralleled by clear indications from developing countries that attitudes towards foreign direct investment are in a state of flux. The rhetoric used has changed, definitely. Heated debates over alleged or real imperialistic exploitation of developing countries' economies by multinational corporations have ebbed and given way to a more realistic assessment of the merits and disadvantages of direct investments. Governments of developing countries compete for foreign direct investment on an international scale (as do industrialized countries for selected industries, too), and it is very rare to hear those far-reaching reservations against foreign participation in industrial production such as were expressed in the sixties and seventies and which materialized in extremely restrictive investment policies. There are clear moves towards liberalizing foreign investment regulations, partly by changing laws and decrees, partly by a more liberal interpretation of existing regulations.

Up to 1985, investment flows had not yet responded forcefully to this changing environment. According to International Monetary Fund statistics the net flow of direct investment to indebted developing countries fell from its peak of 14 billion dollars in 1981 to 9,1 billion in 1984.[1] First estimates for 1985 indicate that it has stabilized in the range of 9 to 10 billion dollars. Although these figures indicate a decline in foreign direct investment they may be interpreted more optimistically. Firstly, transferred earnings are traditionally more stable than retained or reinvested earnings. The sharp decline in profitability due to the severe recession of the 1980s has fallen overproportionately on retained earnings which constitute a sizable proportion of foreign direct investment. The decline in net investment figures is, to some extent, a cyclical phenomenon which might be reversed if economic conditions on developing countries' domestic and export markets ameliorate. Secondly, although the net flow of foreign direct investment capital has declined, it has done so much less than the amount of new bank credits. It has gained in relative importance and has proven to be a more stable source of external finance.

Nevertheless, foreign direct investment flows are inadequate if measured by their potential contribution to the industrialization and economic growth of developing countries. Many of these have ample natural resources, a growing reservoir of skilled labour and low consumption standards – opportunities for profitable investment which might be seized by foreign investors.

There is a wide gap between declared intentions to reap potential benefits from foreign direct investment for economic growth and adjustment in developing countries and the actual behaviour of foreign direct investment flows. Foreign direct investment could and should play a more important rôle in the financing of development needs: this is a widely shared belief among political leaders from developing and developed countries alike, representatives of international organizations like World Bank and International Monetary Fund, and members of the economics profession. It was also the driving motivation for the Swiss Institute for Research into International Economic Relations, Economic Structures and Regional Science to organize an international symposium at the St. Gall Graduate School of Economics, Law, Business and Public Administration on the topic of «Promotion and Protection of Foreign Private Investment in Developing Countries» on November 12th and 13th 1985. Leading experts from developing countries' investment authorities, from interna-

---

[1] International Monetary Fund, World Economic Outlook, Washington, 1985, appendix table 38.

tional organizations, and from investing European firms, discussed prospects and opportunities for strengthening direct investment flows to developing countries. This volume collects together all the lectures given at the Symposium. Discussions, especially those which were held bilaterally or within small groups, have not been recorded. This publication, then, gives only a partial account of the deliberations, and I should like to add: it offers a partial but representative record of opinions and conclusions.

For the rest of these introductory remarks I will try to highlight some main areas of understanding which were reached during the conference. It is a personal interpretation of the deliberations, and I do not strive for a summary which is accurate in every detail.

Inadequate Structure of External Finance

Compared to historical standards there was a marked shift in the structure of international financing for development which started in the late sixties: away from official to private financing, away from equity to debt investments, and, within the latter, away from securities to bank credits with increasingly shorter maturities and floating interest rates. It is by now commonly agreed that this financing structure has unfavourable risk characteristics. Formally, debtor nations assumed more and more of the economic risks involved, without really being able and willing to carry them when economic conditions worsened. Worldwide economic recession in the early eighties, rising real interest rates and falling relative prices for many debtor country's exports led to a wide-spread inability to honor fiscal obligations. The debt crisis has brought back to the international banking system the economic risks involved in financing general balance of payments needs.

The heavy reliance on bank credits has unfavourable risk characteristics for crediting nations too. Because secondary markets are practically inexistent, risk diversification is restricted and adjustment of portfolios to the evolution of perceived risks is extremely difficult. Banks are caught with large amounts of involuntarily held assets. This situation renders the international financial system vulnerable to external shocks (oil price increases for oil importing debtors or falling oil prices for oil exporting countries) and makes it extremely difficult for it to return to voluntary lending. As long as outstanding credits do not correspond to an optimal portfolio (measured in terms of perceived risks and returns) voluntary new net lending will not be forthcoming. Securing a stable flow of external finance to indebted developing countries will be a very difficult task, as is illustrated by the discussions following the announcement of the Baker Plan in October 1985. The Baker Plan calls for an increase of the outstanding debt to the 15 most heavily indebted nations by two to three per cent annually and is linked to far-reaching market oriented adjustment programs. These figures are smaller than inflation rates in the currencies involved and compared to annual growth rates of 15 to 20 per cent in the late seventies without corrective policy interventions. The issue of international development financing will be severely blocked as long as the banking system is caught with large amounts of involuntarily held credits.

The reasons for this unfortunate development are fairly well understood – with the benefit of hindsight. It may, nevertheless, be worthwhile recalling some basic features, because a clear diagnosis is helpful in shaping therapy.

Firstly, there was a wide-spread misunderstanding of the problems caused by the two oil price increases. It was very unfortunate that the expression «recycling» had been coined. It fostered the illusion that reshuffling of liquidity was the problem. Indeed, banks did a good job in transferring liquidity from oil exporting countries with low domestic absorption to oil importing developing countries, and assuming the risks involved. The real problem, however, was one of adjusting economies to external shocks. External financing can only be a means of smoothing the necessary adjustment to severe external shocks, not one of postponing adjustment. This basic truth got partly lost in the preoccupation with «recycling».

Secondly, it was not well understood that private credits to sovereign states combine the negative characteristics of securities and credits to private customers. Creditors are locked into the relation without having the opportunity to seize real assets in case of default or to influence management decisions if economic conditions turn out badly. Securities share the second characteristic, but the individual investor keeps the flexibility to adjust his portfolio to a change in perceived risks. Inflexibility of credits to private customers is usually compensated by remedies in case of default.

The relative decline of equity financing in the seventies referred to by several authors (cf. Sommaruga, Hegewisch, Alejo)[1] may be partly explained by the explosion of outstanding bank credits, an evolution

[1] Reference is made to articles collected in this volume.

which will certainly not be repeated in coming years. But, thirdly, it has also to do with regulations which severely restricted direct investments but put rarely any restrictions on debt instruments (cf. Hegewisch on this point). Restrictions concerning target industry, firm size, participation quota, nationality of management personnel, technology involved, strategic marketing decisions, transfer of earnings and capital, price controls which can be used for creeping expropriation are illustrations of this development. Regulation of competing financial instruments was certainly biased in favour of debt instruments and to the detriment of equity financing which would have had better risk characteristics.

Strategic Variable: Stability of Investment Regulation

Alternative sources of financing have been drying up and will not become rich springs for development finance again within the coming years. If highly indebted developing countries want to retain some minimal level of voluntary private financing for development programs, they have no choice but to adopt a more sanguine attitude towards foreign direct investment. This does not mean that government should abandon all regulations on foreign investment and enter the competition for potential investors with the whole array of fiscal and regulatory incentives. This would mean falling into the other extreme position and is to a large degree self-defeating if all countries compete on these same terms (cf. Sommaruga).

Using such incentives as a means of attracting long-term investment reflects also a wide-spread misjudgment of strategic variables for private enterprise. Incentives which are tailored to the specific situation and which, very often, are at the discretion of bureaucratic authorities lead to great uncertainty regarding future investment policies as long as constitutional protection of property rights is weak as is often the case in developing countries. Short-term incentives coupled with uncertainty regarding basic principles of future protection of private investment do not meet the strategic needs of private business. They are of little effect at best, but are more likely to bias foreign investment towards footloose industries and, hence, expose the host country to the vagaries of small cost differentials.

A stable and predictable legal and political environment is much more important for investment decisions. Special incentives can complement but not substitute for credible investment regulations. As long as regulations are predictable they can even be restrictive if markets offer opportunities.

Consistent and stable policies affecting the economic viability of an investment are the basis for long-term cooperation (Maucher).

I think that few people would seriously dispute this proposition. Nevertheless, it is difficult to overcome a sense of basic uncertainty when thinking of most developing countries. Constitutional tradition in questions of property rights is usually weak; most developing countries have a long record of leaving great discretionary margins for market interventions and controls to bureaucracies who may suddenly be out of office following a change in political power; without strong constitutional controls predictability of policies is a question of the credibility of government intentions and this is built up by a record of past experience. Only few developing countries have already such a record of stable policies governing foreign direct investment. I am convinced that many other countries are trying to build up this asset, but it takes time to change expectations regarding the credibility of policy actions.

Constitutional Function of International Commitments

Weak constitutional restraints on policies affecting the economic viability of investments and a low record of long-term stability are a good basis from which to discuss the economic function of international commitments and of the involvement of international organizations. They are effective only if they succeed in making policies more predictable and more stable by restricting the discretionary margin of governments. In so doing they have a constitutional function. Constitutions are a means of self-restraint to foster credibility of policy commitments. International agreements and organizations have their best long-term effect on investment flows if they are conceived in this same spirit.

Attributing constitutional functions to institutions like Investment Protection Treaties, the International Centre for the Settlement of Investment Disputes (ICSID), or the Multilateral Investment Guarantee Agency (MIGA) helps to clarify basic issues. Firstly, they contribute to a stronger flow of equity capital to developing countries only if they imply some form of self-restraint regarding future policy change. National treatment, guarantees for the transfer of earnings and capital and arbitration clauses which are basic provisions of existing investment protection treaties (Burkhardt) are a good illustration of this point. Basic material provisions (national treatment, guarantees for transfer) have to be combined with procedural rules (diplomatic negotiations, or reference to ICSID arbitration) so as to enhance the probability that commitments are honored. To link investment insurance to the existence of investment protection treaties as is done by the German scheme (Wurmstich) has the same effect. It gives those host countries eager to attract foreign investment an incentive to conclude and to honor investment protection treaties and helps to reduce uncertainty regarding their future investment policy.

Similar arguments hold for MIGA. If conceived primarily as an insurance agency MIGA would certainly be confronted with the problems of adverse risk selection and would potentially induce host countries to reduce their level of investment protection because investors and host countries could transfer risks to an international organization. The private insurance industry can provide flexible cover for shorter maturities, but it cannot insure against political risk for longer periods at fixed premiums (Radcliffe). Nor could MIGA do without additional provision. It is not a cosmetic but a substantive factor that insurance is only a part of the MIGA proposal and that much weight is given to the policy dialogue regarding investment regulation (Shihata). MIGA can succeed best in promoting private investment flows to developing countries if it succeeds in fostering the credibility of host countries' investment policies.

Discussing international investment treaties and organizations as functionally equivalent to constitutional restraints puts into sharp focus, secondly, their very sensitive political nature. Both are aimed at binding discretionary policy decisions. It is understandable that the fear of foreign interference with national sovereignty looms large in these issues. Initiatives have to strike a delicate balance between respecting national sovereign rights on the one hand and securing a more stable and predictable investment climate for foreign investors on the other. Banning investment controls entirely or focusing solely on investment protection without any regard to internal investment régimes is unbalanced as is the doctrine of some Latin American countries that national treatment is not compatible with treating foreign investors better than their own nationals (e.g. in granting access to international arbitration to foreign but not to local investors).

A strong constitutional order which is conducive to private investment (legal security of property rights, market oriented economic constitution) would certainly be the best solution and would not be subject to the politically sensitive questions of sovereignty. In its absence, some second best solutions have to be found, which provide greater stability and do not interfere unnecessarily with developing countries' policies.

MIGA has some features which are promising in this respect (cf. Shihata). It is part of the World Bank Family and is firmly anchored in an international institution with a good reputation and a history of accepted policy dialogue. It aims at a balanced participation of host and home countries alike, and developing countries have a relatively strong representation compared to the general structure of the Bretton Woods Institutions. It must cover its cost by receipts, which means that it has to achieve a better indemnity record than the private insurance industry if it really wants to grant long-term cover at fixed or nearly fixed rates. This provides a strong incentive for a policy dialogue with developing countries – and such a dialogue is apt to contribute to a better investment climate.

Direct Investment and Technology Transfer

Direct investments transfer a bundle of resources: capital, technical know-how, management skills, marketing knowledge. Transfer of economically valuable information – technology transfer in its broadest definition – is inherently involved with the issue of direct investment. Indeed, the latter cannot be discussed adequately without taking issues of technology transfer into account.

Evaluating technology transfer requires an answer to three basic questions: Who shall decide what technologies should be applied, the market or some governmental agency? What technology and which mode of transfer have the best cost-benefit relation? What factors contribute best to an effective absorption of economically valuable information into the stock of knowledge of the host economy? These are very broad questions which go beyond foreign direct investment but are of special relevance for it. I will take up some of the most pertinent issues.

Markets react to profit opportunities. This general proposition applies also to technology markets. The question of who shall decide comes down to a social evaluation of opportunities for private profits. This in turn depends heavily on the set of restraints under which private economic agents decide to allocate scarce resources. Economists hold that profit opportunities indicate social value if market access is not overly restricted and if one accepts the distribution of factor endowments. There is no reason why it should be radically different for developing countries. It is also the basic assumption for investment decisions of the International Finance Corporation (IFC). IFC offers advice, partial financing and risk taking, and the «umbrella-function» of an international organization to

facilitate a more effective exploitation of existing opportunities for profitable investment in developing countries (Alejo, Pollan) – as investors attest with a reasonable record of success (cf. Amstutz and Huber). The doubling of IFC's working capital and the move towards a more aggressive policy stance by IFC management (Alejo) signal the fact that the World Bank Group is inclined to support profit seeking activities for development.
Nonetheless, there remains a strong involvement of developing countries' governments in the economic process. Even though there is a tendency towards greater reliance on private business, state enterprises play an important rôle and most governments have some form of licence procedure for foreign investments. These facts cannot be denied and must be respected. IFC projects are worked out in cooperation with host countries' governments (otherwise it would be extremely difficult to secure the umbrella-function); national insurance schemes require the approval of the host government before insurance cover is extended (Wurmstich); the same holds true for the MIGA proposal (Shihata).I think it is correct to concede to host governments the decision whether a foreign investment should be started. But it must be emphasized that approved projects can only operate successfully if entrepreneurs have some minimal flexibility regarding strategic business decisions (products, pricing, production processes).

Entrepreneurial flexibility can be accorded more easily if basic prerequisites for competitive markets are given, namely low barriers to entry and unbiased and flexible prices. To illustrate the second point by an example: If interest rate ceilings and import subsidies for capital goods (direct subsidies or overvalued exchange rates coupled with import preferences for machinery) bias relative factor prices in favour of capital intensive technologies, private profit seeking activities will result in production processes which do not respect the local requirement for labor-intensive technologies. Government interference with decisions on production processes may be justified by the need to meet social objectives – more effective, however, would be to reduce government interventions on factor markets, so that relative prices really correspond to the relative scarcity of labor and capital. The call for government actions to correct market failures is more often than not a call to correct the market effects of previous interventions.

In the context of technology transfer issues foreign direct investment raises the question of bundling vs. unbundling. There was a time when the argument was put forward strongly that unbundling the flow of resources would lower the aggregate cost to developing countries. Technology should be bought on world markets by agreements like licensing, management contracts, long-term sales contracts and capital provided separately on international capital markets. There are certainly instances where unbundling is feasible and has better cost-benefit characteristics. This may apply especially when the rights of ownership at intangible assets are easily enforced and the receiving partner has a high capacity to absorb and to adapt existent technologies to local needs.

As a general proposition, the call for unbundling has lost ground and direct investments are generally evaluated more favourably than before. The basic argument is to be found in the growing recognition that technology transfer is not a one-off deal but requires a steady stream of new information. Technology transfer is inherently a learning process. Information must effectively be absorbed by people if it is really to be transferred from one country to another. The integration into the information network of an international enterprise offers opportunities for learning processes which are absent in an arm's length bargaining situation. This holds especially true if an orientation towards integrating local personnel is a strategic decision of a multinational enterprise (Maucher).

Mutual Interest in Long-Term Cooperation

With the exception of footloose industries which produce for export markets and have low capital requirements and which can, therefore, easily change location, direct investments are long-term commitments. Foreign investors do not only bear responsibility for but also have a long-term interest in a balanced development of a host country's economy and society. The more an investment contributes to achieving the economic and social objectives of the host country the better is its long-term economic viability, regardless of changing political environments. Changing attitudes towards a better understanding of opportunities for mutual interest on both the investors' and the host countries' side (Maucher) might be the most far-reaching policy objective in the field of foreign direct investment. Fiscal incentives, insurance against non-commercial risks, pleas for increased flows of equity capital by international organizations: all these can complement but not substitute for favourable attitudes towards international cooperation between private business and developing countries which take into account each partner's long-term interests.

Aussenwirtschaft, 41. Jahrgang (1986), Heft I, Grüsch: Rüegger, S.19–23

Opening Address

Dr. Cornelio Sommaruga
State Secretary, Berne

The topic of foreign direct private investment is characterized by vast literature, countless seminars and heated debates. One may wonder why the University of St. Gallen took the initiative of inviting an international audience of such high reputation to discuss it once again and why, Ladies and Gentlemen, you accepted the invitation. Hasn't everthing already been said about private investment? Certainly not!

There was a time when opinion was sharply divided between those who regarded foreign private investment as the panacea for the development problem and those who regarded it to be an instrument for the political and economic exploitation of the developing countries. A superficial view of recent investment figures of the last years could lead to the erroneous conclusion, that the developing countries suppose the exploitation theory to be true. Direct investment in developing countries of the Western Hemisphere, which had attracted well over half of all private capital flows during the 1960's, represented barely one quarter of a much larger volume of such flows by the late 1970's, most of which were accounted for by bank lending or export credits.

I do not need to dwell upon the reasons for the relative decline of investment flows: Recession, the replacement of investments by the banks' liberal lending policy in the 70's, are much too evident. Nevertheless, it is worthwhile noting that during the recent recession of 1981 to 1983, direct investment fell only by 29 per cent, while net borrowing from private creditors fell by 72 per cent.[1]

I am not going to conclude from this comparison that once more there is an increasing awareness of the useful contribution of private investment in the development process of a market-oriented economy. Numerous other and more obvious factors underline this fact, primarily mounting debt burdens and stagnating, if not reduced, aid flows. Today, many developing countries are obliged to pursue a rigorous policy of austerity in

[1] «Foreign Private Investment in Developing Countries», IMF, Occasional Paper 33, Washington, January 1985

order to honour their external debt and to satisfy at the same time the basic needs of the population. But of course, such a drastic policy is in the long run unacceptable for a government anxious to revert to growth. Since the prospects for considerable new foreign lending are slim in the foreseeable future, one of the only realistic ways out for them is to promote investment, including foreign direct investment.

Unlike debt, direct investment requires no service payment unless it earns a return. The higher the proportion of direct investment in the total external liability, the easier therefore the process of adjustment to economic disturbances. For 28 developing countries that have re-scheduled their external debts in 1983, the share of direct investment accounts for an average of only 14 per cent of their total external liabilities, compared with an average of 24 per cent for 49 developing countries which did not have to reschedule their debt. At the same time, one must realize that under favourable economic circumstances an investor will claim a higher rate of return than a bank lender, since the investor's risk is normally higher.

The other advantages of foreign direct investment are well known: Not only does it represent a means to transfer capital from North to South but it is generally linked to productive development plans of internationally competitive enterprises. It can also facilitate the transfer of technology, know-how, marketing and management skills. The more the foreign investment is «integrated» into the national economy of the developing countries, the more beneficial it is for them.

I am inclined to argue that today foreign direct investment is no longer such a controversial issue among serious economists, except if used – or misused – for ideological purposes. In saying this, I do not pretend that all problems related to direct investment are solved. I only mean that these problems are manageable, that developing countries *can* come to grips with their legitimate concern regarding foreign ownership and influence on their economy without at the same time discouraging potential foreign investors from realizing their plans.

This task is certainly not easy. To a certain extent foreign investors can choose from among a number of alternative host country locations. There exists, in effect, a market for foreign investment projects in which host countries compete for market shares. Therefore, a government has to define a foreign investment policy that, on the one hand, maximizes the benefits the host country can derive from direct foreign investment and, on the other hand, permits the firms to get a return on their investment commensurate with their entrepreneurial risk.

Furthermore, a country also has to take into account the investment strategy followed by its neighbours if it wants to remain competitive. Over time this has led to a catalogue – still expanding today – of incentives to promote foreign investment. Investment subsidies, tax holidays, tax reductions and accelerated depreciation allowances are among the best known examples.

Some members of the audience here are more competent than I to judge whether these incentives are really decisive for the location of investment. However, from discussions I had with managers of different firms, I am inclined to think that their introduction may not have fulfilled the expected goals. On the contrary, they have often proved to be both expensive and ineffective; this seems especially true the more complex and the more frequently altered these incentives are. One should not forget, finally, that incentives can provoke a distortion of comparative cost, in the short run beneficial to one country while detrimental to the other. The injured country is then obliged to react by granting similar incentives, so that in the end everybody is again on the same footing but on a «higher» level.

Far more important for investor decisions than incentives are the market size, the growth potential, the overall economic environment a host country can offer together with such favorable conditions as a bureaucracy that is not to heavy and, eminently, sound financial and exchange rate policies.

Another more institutional evolution could also facilitate investment flows to developing countries: I am alluding to the perception of political risks that prevents investors from availing themselves of investment opportunities. Bilateral investment guarantee schemes can notably improve the investment climate by acknowledging the principle of fair and non-discriminatory treatment, and establishing rules in case of nationalization as well as procedures for the settlement of disputes.

In this respect, I think that the renewed life and vigour the World Bank has put into the old idea of creating a multilateral investment guarantee scheme was a timely initiative. No doubt the recently created new institution known under the abbreviation MIGA which was approved in October 1985 by the Governors of the IBRD in Seoul can be an useful instrument for stimulating an increased flow of investment into developing countries and for improving the investment climate in third world countries in the interest of private investor and host country alike.

Up to this point I have dealt mostly with the responsibility of host countries wanting to attract investments. Let me now turn to the investing countries. In an interdependent world, their responsibility is becoming increasingly important, be it on the level of private enterprise or of the government.

In addition to the «traditional» responsibility private enterprises bear – mainly to behave in conformity with the national laws and regulations of the host country – there are two other factors that are not new but that have recently come into the foreground of the development debate.

The first is related to new technologies. No doubt high technology will considerably influence not only comparative advantages but also our way of life, our culture, education and employment. It is certainly too early to assess yet all the modifications the new technologies will bring about, in particular with respect to the last-mentioned element – employment. But I would predict the argument that capital-intensive techniques are inappropriate to labour-rich and capital-scarce developing countries will rise tremendously in importance. These countries might find themselves in a dilemma, either of accepting the new techniques or deepening further the economic trench between North and South. It will be the responsibility primarily of foreign enterprises to show that new technologies need not adversely influence employment and that investment will contribute to job creating policies necessary to absorb a steadily growing population.

The second factor is obvious and does not need long explanation. It relates to environment. The reputation of our transnational enterprises suffers enormously, when accidents happen like those we have witnessed in developed and developing countries during the last few years. They must be avoided at all costs.

The government also has its role to play in favouring investment flows. In most developed countries, there is a lobby of opinion urging closer monitoring of foreign investment on the ground that it has resulted in exporting jobs. This is not true! Most studies on the subject have concluded that such investment does not lead to a net loss of employment in the capital exporting country, once the indirect effects on employment as well as the increased exports generated by direct investments are included. It is only proper, then, that governments have in general resisted that kind of lobby.

Unfortunately, I cannot say the same of protectionism. Although the protectionist wave we are currently experiencing is not directly aimed at reducing direct investment flows, it often discourages new export-oriented investments in those sectors, in which developing countries have the greatest comparative advantage. Protectionism is most unfortunate. It deprives the successful entrepreneur of the fruit of his efforts; worse, it undermines the credibility of market economy. The greatest contribution governments of developed countries could make towards fostering investment flows to developing countries would be to resist protectionist pressures and to roll back the ones already in effect, in short: to secure access to world markets.

I have now concluded my remarks. Of course, there are developments other than those I mentioned, which advocate a serious discussion on foreign private investment. And I hope, that you will be able to deal with them. Let me therefore express the desire, also in the name of the Federal Council, that the coming debates cast a new light on these difficult problems and contribute to their better understanding and consequently to their solution. Let me conclude by expressing my thanks and appreciation to the University of St. Gallen and to its Institute for Research into International Economic Relations, Economic Structures and Regional Science for having taken the initiative to assemble us here.

Part I

Trade and Investment: The Importance of Foreign Private Investment for Development

Aussenwirtschaft, 41. Jahrgang (1986), Heft I, Grüsch: Rüegger, S. 27–36

Trade, Debt and Investment: The Importance of Foreign Private Investment for Development

Dr. C. Fred Bergsten
Director, Institute for International Economics, Washington

The Imperatives for Development

There are three crucial requirements for a resumption of self-sustained growth in the developing world: further changes in the policies of the developing countries themselves, and substantial increases in both the quantity and quality of external resources made available to them. None of the three is likely without the other two, so they form an internally consistent set of measures calling for cooperative action by the governments and private sectors of both the industrial and developing countries.

The Quantity of External Capital

The developing countries (LDCs) have already adjusted substantially to their debt crisis. The current account deficit of the LDCs, taken together, peaked at more than $100 billion in 1981 and was cut in half by 1983–84. It is conceivable that they could hold their joint external deficit within this range while resuming rapid internal growth, as Brazil has already done. It is also conceivable that external finance of this magnitude could be made available from existing sources without further policy changes.

However, such a «stand pat» strategy would entail substantial risks for several reasons. First, the commercial banks are balking at providing any new credits to the LDCs, let alone their $15–20 billion «share» of any total external financing package of $50 billion or so.

Moreover, the deficits of the LDCs could rise substantially even without any relaxation of their own adjustment efforts. A recession in the OECD countries, or even a «growth recession» with economic expansion limited to 2 percent or less, would produce inadequate growth in world trade to enable LDCs to earn the increased foreign exchange needed to continue servicing this debt without facing renewed recessions at home. Increased protectionism in the industrial countries, a particular threat in the United States in light of the continued overvaluation of the dollar and massive trade deficit, could also stifle LDC export expansion. A sharp move in the oil price in either direction, but particularly downward in light of the greater impact of such changes on oil exporters than oil importers, could also worsen the picture substantially.[1]

In addition, the current account positions of the LDCs will inevitably be hurt by the coming correction of at least a large part of the American external deficit. That deficit will approximate $125 billion for 1985, and could be even higher in 1986. Perhaps $15 billion of the American deterioration from 1980–81 to 1985–86 stemmed from the LDCs' adjustment to their debt crisis,[2] and they will unfortunately feel at least some adverse impact from the essential American adjustment of $100 billion or so over the remainder of the decade.

Furthermore, it would be highly desirable to «buy» more rapid economic growth in the developing world if effective means could be found for doing so. The humanitarian case for increasing living standards in this huge part of the world provides adequate justification for such an effort. In addition, a resumption of self-sustaining growth may be essential to assure continued LDC cooperation in responding to the debt crisis and to encourage LDC governments to maintain their adjustment efforts.

The traditional rule of thumb is that an extra $10–15 billion of external finance can support an additional 1 percentage point of economic growth in the developing world. My colleagues Donald Lessard and John Williamson have recently produced a more sophisticated calculation, posited on the view that the key current constraint on expansion in most LDCs is a shortage of foreign exchange rather than of domestic savings. Because of this constraint, production and growth – not just consumption and other domestic absorption – are being limited. This problem is particularly acute in the short term, because it takes time to develop and implement the expenditure-switching (and thus export-led growth) strategies which are the only basic answer for the long term.[3] In addition, increased foreign exchange inflows would help attack the other major con-

---

[1] A complete model of these effects can be found in William R. Cline, *International Debt: Systemic Risk and Policy Response,* Washington, Institute for International Economics, 1984, especially Chapter 3.

[2] See Stephen Marris, *Deficits and the Dollar: The World Economy at Risk,* Washington, Institute for International Economics, December 1985, page 3.

[3] See Donald R. Lessard and John Williamson, *Financial Intermediation Beyond the Debt Crisis,* Washington, Institute for International Economics, September 1985.

straint in many LDCs today, inflation, by permitting a greater influx of foreign goods and appreciation (or less depreciation) of their currencies.

At the same time, it is vitally important for the heavily indebted LDCs to continue to reduce their debt-export ratios and thus return toward market creditworthiness. Modest movement in this direction is occurring now; indeed, this is the desirable side of the current net outward transfer of resources from many LDCs. Such long-run progress will continue even with some increase in external capital flows over the presently envisaged levels, however, so this concern should not deter efforts to expand such flows.

These considerations argue for a modest but important increase in net capital flows to the developing world at this time: to hedge against the inevitable uncertainties surrounding both the supply and demand sides of the world economy, and to encourage more rapid growth in the LDCs by helping alleviate their foreign exchange constraint. Lessard and Williamson calculate that a sustainable borrowing level for the LDCs as a group is now about $80 billion annually, as compared with a maximum likely availability of $50 billion. An increase of $30 billion in annual flows, however, even if attainable, could push debt-export ratios up again. Thus, they conclude that a prudent level of increase would be on the order of $15–20 billion annually. This would permit additional output of perhaps $100 billion per year.[1]

The «Baker plan», by contrast, calls for only about $10 billion of increased capital flow per year. It is not even clear that this entire amount would be truly additional, because some of it might simply represent a resumption of bank lending at levels already assumed (about $15 billion annually) in the Lessard-Williamson calculation. One imperative for development is thus increased external capital flow to the LDCs, if their policies assure that the funds will be put to productive use.

The Quality of External Capital

The mix of external capital flows to the LDCs has changed dramatically over the past two decades. Prior to the first oil shock in 1973, about 75 percent of all such flows came from public sources. Of the 25 percent that came from private sources, over half represented foreign direct investment.

---

[1] See *Financial Intermediation Beyond the Debt Crisis,* especially pp. 27–28.

After 1973, the public-private sector mix was reversed. About three quarters of all such flows were now private. Of that private total, only about one quarter was in the form of direct investment.

The big change, of course, came from the huge increase in commercial bank «recycling» of petrodollars. Unfortunately, such bank loans were peculiarly unsuited to the needs of the borrowing developing countries. Most were at quite short maturities. Most carried floating interest rates. Few bore any relationship to the ability of the borrower to pay, either in terms of particular projects or of overall national performances.

It is clear that the future structure of international capital transfers needs to be reformed to avoid recreating these shortcomings. The time profile of the transfers should relate to the country's ability to pay. There should be meaningful sharing of the risks of individual projects.[1]

There are thus three central requirements for enhancing the contribution of external capital to LDC development in the coming years. First, the annual flow needs to be greater by perhaps $15–20 billion (and conceivably even $30 billion). Second, the public and private shares of these flows should probably be about equal – representing a synthesis between the opposite (and lopsided) mixes of pre-1973 and post-1973. Third, the quality of the flow needs to be greatly improved by the use of new techniques for both public and, especially, private flows as explored below.

LDC Policies

Before exploring those specific ideas, however, it is essential to stress the critical importance of effective LDC development strategies and policies. Larger and more diversified external capital flows neither will, nor should, be made available without reasonable assurance that they will be used effectively. The record of various LDCs on this score differs dramatically over the past two decades, offering both hope for progress and discouragement over the prospects in some cases.

The basic objective, especially for LDCs now saddled with heavy external debt, must be to simultaneously restore self-sustaining growth and maintain internal and external stability. In turn, the only feasible technique to this end is the adoption, or maintenance where already adopted, of market-based and outward-oriented policies. In particular, a combina-

---

[1] These considerations are elaborated in *Financial Intermediation Beyond the Debt Crisis*, especially Chapter 3.

tion of export expansion and efficient import-substitution is crucial; only with such a thrust can countries both continue to service their external debt responsibility (by earning and saving the needed foreign exchange) *and* achieve lasting economic growth (through the pull of exports on the entire economy).[1]

The three imperatives for development cited here – improved LDC policies, greater quantities and better quality of external capital flows – are the central components of the «Baker plan». That proposal is best viewed as a stretching out over time of the three main themes of the global response to the debt problem which has been in place since the crisis broke in mid-1982: the debtor countries must now adopt structural and lasting economic reforms rather than «simply» short-run demand compression, the IBRD with its long-run growth and development emphasis will play a relatively greater role than the IMF with its inherently short-run focus on stability (and the BIS with its very short-term rescue packages), and the commercial banks need to work out multiyear reschedulings and commit new money for several years at a time rather than operating solely on an annual basis. The approach is still case-by-case, but clearly with the view that resolution of the problem will take many years so that more lasting strategies are needed. The «Baker plan» is thus a move in the right direction though, as noted, it does not go nearly far enough to meet the needs of the latter half of the 1980s.

The Role of Private Foreign Investment

Private foreign investment can contribute substantially to each of these three requirements. With proper LDC policies and inducements, it can add – perhaps substantially – to the total availability of external resources. Undertaken in proper forms, it can significantly improve the quality of such transfers. And it can make an important contribution to export-led growth policies in the LDCs themselves, which in turn would promote still more inflow and thus generate a virtuous cycle of potentially enormous importance to the future of those countries.

---

[1] A useful summary of this strategy can be found in Bela Balassa, «Outward Orientation», *Handbook for Development Economics,* Hollis B. Chenery and P.N. Srinivasan, editors, North Holland, Amsterdam, forthcoming. An application of this strategy to Latin America is developed in Bela Balassa, Gerardo Bueno, Pedro Pablo Kuczynski, and Mario Henrique Simonsen, *Toward a New Development Strategy for Latin America,* Washington, Institute for International Economics, June 1986.

Portfolio Investments

There are numerous types of private (nonbank) foreign investment which can contribute to such outcomes. One is foreign direct investment, to which I return below for more detailed discussion. But there are also a variety of channels for increasing portfolio flows. Their goal is essentially to tap the huge reservoir of investment capital now being generated by institutional investors – notably insurance companies, pension funds and mutual funds – in the United States, Japan and other industrial countries. The total capitalization of world financial markets probably now exceeds $ 15 trillion and is expanding by at least $ 1 trillion annually. Even a relatively tiny redirection of those funds to LDCs could make an enormous contribution to the development objective.

Techniques for attracting some of these funds to LDCs could include the expansion and deepening of equity markets in the countries themselves, combined with regulatory changes to improve the climate for (or at least permit) foreign purchases: encouragement of real estate investment; issuance of indexed and commodity-linked bonds; quasi-equities such as revenue sharing and production sharing contracts; and perhaps special repatriation funds to reverse capital flight. Lassard and Williamson describe and analyze these techniques in some detail, and suggest that each could generate an extra $ 1–2 billion of capital flows annually.[1] It will take some time to do so, however, and meanwhile the public international institutions (especially the World Bank) and the commercial banks will have to fill the gap as much as possible. Again, the importance of sound LDC policies to stimulate such flows cannot be overemphasized.

Foreign Direct Investment

Foreign direct investment can play a particularly useful, even critical, role within this broader framework of LDC needs and private capital opportunities. Such investment inherently links the return on the invested capital to the actual performance of both the specific project financed and the host country as a whole. Returns rise when performance is good, hence enabling such returns to be transferred. Returns fall when a project or overall economy falters, thus providing a countercyclical stabilization of great benefit to the host country. The enormous financial impact of the global recession of 1982 could have been muted, and the entire debt crisis perhaps averted, if a significant share of the recycling of the 1970s had taken the form of direct investment rather than short-maturity, floating-rate bank loans.

---

[1] See *Financial Intermediation Beyond the Debt Crisis,* especially Chapter 5.

In addition, foreign direct investment can directly support export-led, outward-oriented growth strategies in the developing countries. Both the technologies and marketing skills of multinational firms substantially abet the export performance of LDC host countries (assuming of course that internal practices of the firms do not deter such exports, or that LDC policies prohibit any such limitations). Another contribution of multinationals to LDC export efforts is that they can resist, often decisively, protectionist pressures in their home countries which could deny market access to the LDC products in question and thus jeopardize an entire outward-oriented development strategy.[1]

Unfortunately, the level of new foreign direct investment in the developing countries has been falling steeply: from $14 billion in 1981 to $9 billion in 1984, with 80 percent of the decline occuring in Latin America.[2] Some experts expect a modest cyclical pickup in 1985–86, with an increase of perhaps 8 percent in 1985–86 and then a «more normal» expansion of 3–4 percent beyond (as during 1967–84 as a whole). This would bring the actual level of new foreign direct investment, in real terms, back to the previous peak (1981) in 1989. Even this «normal» prospect would mean that foreign direct investment was again financing about one quarter of the total projected LDC current account deficit in the latter 1980s, approaching its share of the pre-1973 period; for the heavily indebted LDCs, foreign direct investment would probably be playing an even greater role than its traditional 10–15 percent.

The issue, however, is whether policy and attitudinal changes in both host and home countries could enable foreign direct investment to make an even greater contribution in the future. The potential is clearly substantial. Production is increasingly globalized. Numerous LDCs are attractive to multinational investors because of their capability to provide an efficient base for servicing global sales. The markets of many developing countries, particularly in East Asia but also in Latin America despite its current difficulties, are likely to grow rapidly. Survey evidence indicates and underlying interest in investing in many of these countries even at the height of the debt crisis.[3]

---

[1] C. Fred Bergsten, Thomas Horst, and Theodore H. Moran, *American Multinationals and American Interests,* Washington, The Brookings Institution, 1978, erspecially Chapter 8.

[2] These and most of the subsequent numbers cited are taken from IMF, *World Economic Outlook,* 1985, Appendix Table 38; IMF, *Foreign Direct Investment in Developing Countries,* Occasional Paper 33, January 1985; and David J. Goldsbrough, «Past Trends and Prospects for Foreign Direct Investment in Developing Countries: The Link With Bank Lending», unpublished, 1985.

[3] Group of Thirty, *Foreign Direct Investment 1973–1987,* New York, 1985.

It is thus relevant to assess the nature of policy changes that might encourage maximum realization of these interests and important to note that many such changes have already taken place. Countries ranging from Argentina through Brazil and Mexico to India have significantly altered traditional policies which have deterred foreign direct investment. After years of indecision, the membership of the World Bank has approved a Multilateral Investment Guarantee Agency (MIGA) to insure foreign direct investment and improve the investment climate more generally, and a number of LDCs appear likely to sign and ratify its charter. The United States has joined several European countries in negotiating Bilateral Investment Treaties (BITs) with selected LDCs in pursuit of similar objectives.

Further changes should proceed in similar directions, but could reasonably go much further. There are two key elements for the developing host countries. One is the adoption of macroeconomic policies which are conducive to efficient and profitable participation by multinational firms: competitive exchange rates, open trade policies, positive real interest rates, effective growth and anti-inflation strategies. The second is the adoption of specific policies toward foreign direct investment which will encourage it to enter and stay: a consistent and credible legal framework, minimization of regulatory red tape and other onerous transactions costs, minimization of performance requirements which distort a company's behavior, and national treatment on the whole range of corporate activities.

One possibility, given the needs of the late 1980s as described above, would be for the international financial institutions (notably the World Bank and Inter-American Development Bank and, to a lesser extent, the IMF) to place high priority on policies supportive of foreign direct investment in fashioning their structural adjustment loans (SALs) and other lending programs. There is much talk of «converting debt to equity» and relying much more heavily on equity finance in the future, but little policy action to that end.

Most of the needed macroeconomic measures are included in SALs and related programs anyway, and attaching priority to foreign direct investment would simply reinforce these inclinations. The main incremental impact would be the extension of International Finance Institute (IFI) lending conditions to include the kinds of investment-specific measures listed above. Doing so would provide a natural complement, and indeed reinforcement, to the trade-liberalizing and investment-promoting components already included in most of these programs.

The developing countries should not resist such conditions too strongly. Many of them developed extensive nationalistic reactions against foreign direct investment in the early 1970s, and as a result had to turn to bank lending to tide them through the oil shocks – lending which, as stated above, was inherently inappropriate to their needs and landed them in the debt crisis which has made the 1980s a «lost decade» for growth in many. The borrowing LDCs can now see that they did not buy much, if any, political autonomy by rejecting the multinationals in favor of the banks. Now that they face a desperate need to attract capital from all sources, having experienced a sharp decline in their inflows from both banks and multinationals, they must surely be prepared to adopt more supportive policies.

Foreign direct investment remains a controversial and emotional issue in many LDCs, however. Moreover, there are already numerous conditions in SALs and other IFI loan packages so that further additions to the list will not be entirely welcome in many LDCs. Hence the industrial home countries should also adopt supportive new policies in this area as part of their overall contributions to the «Baker plan».

In particular, they could offer improved tax incentives for foreign direct investment in LDCs – either all LDCs, or all heavily indebted countries, or at least the poorest countries. Several options exist: extending the investment tax credit to these countries (as proposed by the Kennedy Administration in the United States and actually negotiated with several countries, but never ratified by the Senate), tax sparing (as proposed and negotiated under the Eisenhower Administration, but also rejected by the Senate) or a tax preference tailored directly to today's conditions. It should be noted that the Reagan Administration proposed a new tax incentive for US investment in the Caribbean countries as part of its Caribbean Basin Inititative, but the idea did not survive the Congressional process.

It would be particularly important for such supportive policies to be adopted in Japan. For the past few years and for the foreseeable future, Japan will be by far the world's largest source of net investment capital. The outflow of long-term capital from Japan has been averaging about $75 billion annually; it will probably remain in this range for at least 1986, and decline but slowly thereafter. Japan is already the world's largest creditor country and its net asset position should approach $500 billion by the end of the decade.

In addition, Japanese companies have begun to globalize their production networks only in the past four years. Most foreign direct investment from Japan in the past has been limited to procuring raw materials or serving other narrowly defined needs of the home islands. With liberalization of capital outflows and an urgent national need to lessen its trade surplus,

Japan has already been rapidly expanding its foreign direct investment and may be poised to do so even more extensively in the years ahead.

One dramatic and perhaps effective way to promote increased foreign direct investment in the developing world would be the creation of a new «GATT for Investment».[1] Its basic purpose, as with the GATT itself, would be to limit government intervention in private decisions in order to improve the climate for foreign direct investment. Such an organization could adopt measures applicable in both home and host countries, and would probably have to incorporate a meaningful code of conduct for the firms themselves to allay fears that any reduction in host-country controls would simply «unleash the powerful multinationals».

Negotiation of such a new set of rules and institutional arrangements would necessarily take some time, given the intellectual complexity of some of the issues and the sensitive politics of foreign direct investment (in home as well as host countries). In conjunction with MIGA and the BITs, however, its launching might be the next logical step in seeking to highlight the importance of foreign private investment for development.

[1] See the update by one of the originators of the idea in Charles P. Kindleberger, *A GATT for Foreign Investment: Further Reflections*, New York, Carnegie Center for Transnational Relations, 1980.

Aussenwirtschaft, 41. Jahrgang (1986), Heft I, Grüsch: Rüegger, S.37–46

Multinational Enterprise and Host Country Policy: Opportunities for Mutual Benefit

Helmut Maucher
Managing Director, Nestlé S.A., Vevey

A few years ago, one of the dominant topics in discussing international economic relations concerned the problems supposed to exist between multinational companies and the host countries.

Meanwhile, the perspective has changed. Without forgetting the still existing negative side effects, we now discuss with our partners inside and outside the host country's governments the basis of the mutual benefit resulting from the cooperation of multinational enterprise and the host countries, and we discuss how to improve this base to increase the mutual benefit.

This new, or at least different approach reflects to a certain degree some *change in attitudes:* A considerable number of developing countries appreciate more and more the positive role of foreign direct investment in their industrialisation process and in their overall economic and social development. Added to which, more and more multinationals have become aware of their responsibility for and their longterm interest in a balanced development of a host country's economy and society.

I shall address myself to two main questions:

Firstly: What are a developing country's main advantages resulting from an inflow of foreign direct investment? Where might consequently multinational enterprise find an area of common interest and mutual benefit to be developed in cooperation with the host country?

Secondly: What should one expect from the host country's policy framework to support the realization of the mutual benefit?

When I use the expression «multinationals» or «foreign direct investment», the reader should be conscious of the fact that this definition comprises a large variety of categories, each equipped with its very own characteristics and interests.

There are, to begin with, *differences in the branch* the enterprises belong to. The activities range from the mainly export oriented raw material production and commercialization to the high tech sector and to food manufacturing and distribution in local markets.

One should also be aware of the fact, that the *traditional north-north and north-south patterns* of multinational activities *are changing:* Foreign direct investment by firms from the Third World, although still less than 3.5 per cent of the world total,[1] by the early 1980s was already having an impact on more than 30 developing countries. There exist also multinational companies owned by the state in centrally planned economies with already some experience as foreign direct investors.

Besides this increasing variety of home countries we observe mounting *differences in the relative importance of home markets:* The share of sales in the domestic market varies from 2%, as in the case of Nestlé in Switzerland, to almost 80% in many U.S. multinationals.

A further point: In some companies there has – for several reasons – taken place a *shift from traditional equity participation to the use of loans and suppliers' credits,* from direct control to management participation, production-sharing, supply contracts, etc. This diversifies further the pattern and the interests of multinational enterprise.

A last important point that should be emphasized here: Considerable *differences* exist *in the actual behaviour* of multinational companies in developing countries, among others, as a result of the number of years of experience in foreign direct investment and also resulting from differences in corporate culture and the basic philosophies behind the enterprises' activities.

Nestlé, for example, had already been active in many countries around the world at a time when expressions such as: «Multis», «Transfer of technology» or «Development Assistance» had not been coined or invented.

Consequently, nobody in this audience will doubt, that the group of companies defined as multinationals has to be considered as highly heterogeneous. Therefore, the search for areas of common interest with host countries needs to be done in a case by case approach. I will do that from the point of view of my experience with Nestlé. I am convinced that some important elements of the case of Nestlé allow for generalizations.

---

[1] ECOSOC; Transnational Corporations in International Trade; Document E/C10/1985/3, Geneva 1985, p. 17.

If the policy of Nestlé is analyzed from a perspective of long-term mutual benefit with host countries, you will find positive effects on three levels: *people, products and systems.*

It is no coincidence when I start with people: As a main principle of our management policy, we are more people and product oriented than systems oriented.

Of course we are aware of the need and the value of systems and methods in a complex organisation. But these systems have to remain operational aids and a guide for us rather than an end in themselves. This is therefore a matter of priority. We consider strong orientation towards people, towards the employee and management to be a very decisive, if not the most decisive component in *long-term* success. This is why we first focus our attention on the choice of managers, as well as on their training and further development, on the relations with our employees and their qualities and training, and the perception of our social responsibilities which, in the long-term, also pay off for the company. The personal and the working climate, a direct and personal management style, the credibility and the reliability of our management and of our relations which reach beyond national frontiers and company units, all these things are of great importance to us. They are the subject of considerable attention and are solidly anchored, especially in the minds of our managers.

In this perspective we do not simply transfer capital and technology to developing countries. We submit knowledge in its broadest sense, and we transfer attitudes, but without imposing any ideology. I will come back to this last point later on.

When we build a new plant in a foreign country, some of our knowledge will be transferred and materialized in a new building and the machinery. After setting up the new factory, further and continuous transfer of knowledge has to take place. As a principle, Nestlé runs its factories abroad with local staff. Mechanics, electricians, accountants, employees and the workers who will keep the factory running must be recruited on the spot. Training at all levels has to be carried out systematically in the factory, on the jobs or through apprenticeships. Technicians and middle managers are trained at specialised local institutes or during short postings to Nestlé factories in other countries.

The result of our effort to transfer knowledge can be demonstrated in the case of a 1961 established milk plant at Moga, India[1]: Despite the

[1] For the history and the economic and social effects of Nestlé's direct investment at Moga see the study: Nestlé in India. The Effects of setting up a factory; Vevey 1985.

increase of overall personnel from 160 in the first year of production to 1293 in the current year, we were able to reduce the international staff from 12 to 3.

But in industry, the transfer of knowledge is no one time shot. After the initial effort a continuous flow of know-how to the people in our subsidiary companies has to initiate and guide improvement and adjustment of products and systems. As a large company with worldwide sales we have the comparative advantage of a combination of two factors: On one side the economies of scale of research and development, and on the other side a broad variety of offered products. Nestlé runs two basic scientific research centres in Switzerland and 18 technological development centres on three different continents. Two of these are located in developing countries to evaluate the local resources and to satisfy local consumers' demands. As in production, the location of research and development of Nestlé is based on a concept of decentralised concentration. All in all we employ more than 3000 people in research and development. Our research centres together with specialised staff from other units – logistics, control, marketing, personal training and so on – enable us to guarantee a *constant transfer* of *know-how* based on the *latest* industrial experience and research results.

In food technology, new developments are not necessarily connected with the so called hi-tech and very dramatic and sensational new ventures. More often, minor modifications in an industrial operation bring about – step by step – additional efficiency and lower cost or improved quality of the final product.

To return to our Moga plant: The continuous transfer of know-how does not stop at the gate of our plants. There are over 35'000 farmers who regularly sell part of their milk production to our subsidiary company at Moga. It is an ongoing task to give them technical advice which, directly or indirectly, will increase their milk production, but not to the detriment of the cultivation of traditional food crops. Our Moga factory set up a free veterinarian service covering the whole district. Other programmes were implemented to improve cattle feeding.

As a result of these programs, the production per buffalo increased from an annual average of 750 kg to 1600 kg per head and year in the case of the best buffaloes. The increase in productivity is limited, primarily due to the traditional buffalo breed in this part of India. The mortality rate for calves, which was 60% in the early sixties, has been reduced to 25%. Again, local tradition that has to be accepted by a multinational as given fact, has hindered further progress. The 25% is made up of male calves. There is no use for them, and they are therefore of no interest to farmers: there is no slaughterhouse in the Punjab, where practically the whole population is vegetarian. At the most one male calf is kept for future reproduction, but all too often the other male calves are left to die of starvation.

The process of constant learning inside and outside our subsidiary companies covers *more than pure production techniques:* Management and logistics, organization and marketing depend on people and their ability to cooperate and adjust their knowledge to new needs.

Multinationals like Nestlé are well suited to transfer an optimum package of know-how directly to the people abroad and to adjust this package continously to new opportunities and new needs. But multinationals do not only transfer their experience to a host country, they learn there, too. There is no doubt that the industrialised world is moving towards the so-called information society. From this altered perspective one should consider a multinational company like Nestlé as a highly efficient international network to exchange information, or, more precisely, knowledge and experience. The effet is a cross-fertilisation of markets on all continents. It takes place indirectly and is systematically organised through the centre, but it is also happening through direct personal contacts. In this latter form, the exchange has more than just an economical dimension: the multinationality of an enterprise might help to *foster mutual understanding between people of different cultures, with different ways of life and of different traditions and beliefs.*

This last point opens our perspective to one more aspect of multinationals in developing countries: Besides the transfer of knowledge there always takes place – to a certain degree – a *transfer of attitudes and philosophy.*

Nestlé is not trying to transfer a closed ideology. We are open to the world and are liberal, and we do not want to force people to adopt our way of life. In general, we tend to have as few uniform policies as possible, to integrate as far as possible with the local situations and mentalities. But on the other hand, one must realize that the host country environment, the attitudes of its people might be positively influenced by certain elements of our «behaviour». When we buy for example milk, we try to get in contact with the efficient and hard working people. We prefer the farmers who are able – if necessary – to increase production and we pay more for higher qualities. In our own interest and – as I'm wholly convinced – not at all to the detriment of our host countries, we demonstrate and disseminate some basic rules of a *free market.* We try more directly to improve – where necessary – *punctuality* and *working discipline* of our labour force, two basic elements of an industrial society in any country.

To return to our Moga factory example: There, Nestlé started at the very beginning of production to organise an efficient system of daily milk collection, to replace the rather improvised system of milk merchants who went from time to time round the villages in search of fresh milk to sell it in town. One effect of these regular milk collections was increased continuity of production and regularity of milk delivery. Again, our behaviour strengthened an attitude – *regularity* – irreplaceable in an efficient economy.

Another aspect of transferred attitudes: *reliability.* The unprecedented regularity with which he is paid for his milk and which he has now observed over a number of years has convinced the farmer producing for our Moga plant that he is not being cheated. One additional remark concerning reliability: It is sometimes said, that foreign investors are unreliable, that they come and go. This is a myth. Once established, foreign direct investment in mining and manufacturing tends to stay even through periods when there are losses. For numerous reasons it is not easy to close a factory and simply leave the country.

Let me at this point briefly sum up the number of people we reach directly and indirectly with our ideas and – more important – with earnings. Moga factory employs directly 1293 persons as well as indirectly some further 450 people. There are over 35'000 farmers who regularly supply the factory with milk. They devote as an average 25% of the farm land to milk production, about 40% of their income come from milk sales. The overall employment and welfare effect of the Moga factory can be regarded as considerable. When I present here the Moga plant as an example, one should keep in mind that Nestlé has 94 industrial operations in 37 LDCs. At the end of 1984 we employed some 50'000 people in developing countries, in other words almost 40 times our staff at Moga factory.

Nestlé is not only people oriented, it is – as an enterprise of the manufacturing industry – also product oriented. Our aim is to serve our customers with products of good quality at a competitive price. We consider this our main justification for doing business, and all we do at the people level is a necessary condition to fulfill this aim.

In developing countries, our policy at the product level follows a kind of double strategy. On the one hand, we use our know-how to produce and sell the usual Western products as far as the consumers there accept them. On the other hand, we develop products which contribute to the improvement of the local nutritional status, which are adequate to eating habits and are based on local raw materials; we offer a good economic price.

We get now to the third level of common interest, the systems.

Developing countries are interested in a growing and diversified manufacturing industry. That is perfectly compatible with the multinationals' desire of decentralized and geographically diversified activities.

Studies of the World Bank and other international organisations show the utmost importance of *efficient investment:* Growth and external debt are only sustainable, if an economy does not waste its resources. The economy needs – on the macro level – a maximal growth effect resulting from the investment. On the micro-economic level, this goes parallel with a good return on investment. Multinational companies are able to realize this return and allocate it – in form of additional investment – in an efficient way.

A further point of common interest on this third – system – level is the *size of plants:* Most developing countries prefer the small and medium sized industries, because of their flexibility. The main bottleneck for their creation seems to be the entrepreneurship: There is a lack of entrepreneurs with the skill, experience, enthusiasm and the financial capacity to provide and combine money, people with adequate knowledge, and machines to build up an efficient factory. Foreign direct investment means in the first place the inflow of entrepreneurial skill; and what follows is in most cases an optimal combination of the necessary production factors. Nestlé systematically uses its entrepreneurial skill and – in its own interest – tries to avoid the negative effects of so-called «gigantism»: we have no large company units; only one factory out of 370 has more than 2000 employees.

In addition: Private direct investment has the advantage of being *the least expensive form,* as it seems not only in comparison with credit but also in comparison with local private investment. It acts as a source of capital, employment, technology, management techniques and other know-how necessary for an efficient economy. It might improve the export potential of a country and it supports the general integration of the host country into the world economy.

To sum up: There is *clear evidence of some positive impact of foreign direct investment* on a developing economy as a result of realized opportunities of mutual benefit. There are also costs. The balance of payments might be influenced, and there are costs as a result of the increased pressure to adjust to the world economy. But we try to avoid as far as possible the negative social and economic side effects, we concentrate on achieving positive effects through cooperation and acting responsibly. Apart from this, government can and does exercise control and impose certain corrective measures.

So, I do not doubt that the cost / benefit balance for both, multinationals *and* host countries, has been positive.

This conclusion is of a certain importance for us: our work is based on long-term cooperation. But any long-term relation will only endure if our activities can be classified as a positive-sum game with equally distributed benefits.

We arrive now at my *second question:* What could and what should host countries do, to support the multinationals in their effort to increase the mutual economic benefit? I do not think, that we can answer this question completely, but I am convinced that multinationals can and should participate more actively and more courageously in the many discussions how to improve the world economy or the situation in a specific country.

I know that what I am saying is dangerous and could be misinterpreted because the political and economical influence of multinationals in certain countries is very often criticised. I do not mean this type of influence which is much exaggerated anyway and always based on the same few cases. Nestlé respects and takes into account not only the legal framework and interests of the countries we work in; we also integrate ourselves with the habits, traditions, mentalities, and unwritten laws of these countries.

What I mean is that we should contribute with our knowledge and international experience; we should express our opinion in negotiations with host countries but also in the many discussions and conferences which take place all over the world. Nobody needs to accept our ideas, but at least they should be heard. We also listen to the ideas expressed by our partners inside and outside the host country's governments and try to learn from their experience.

I have no intention to cover the whole subject, instead I ennumerate here a few points on what host country governments could do to increase common interests and benefit.

We would appreciate it, if the process of replacing ideology through *rational thinking* will continue. Governments and people in the developing world must be aware that ideology and exaggerated nationalism cost a high price in the industrialisation process.

An important element of rational economic policy is *consistency.* If a country expects us to play an important role in its industrialisation concept to increase efficiency, flexibility, production and employment, it might be useful also to reconsider the existing market restrictions in view of their effect on enterprise. With a certain interest, we realized a changing approach of the World Bank experts in their country sector reports. They review the impact of government market interventions on the performance of the food sector of an economy before suggesting general directions in which policy and new programs should move.

In my effort to answer my first question, I mentioned already the importance of regularity and reliability, attitudes essential to any partnership. I should mention here also the *policy stability.* Provision for the renegotiation of contracts and conditions for direct investment should be possible of course, but not come as a surprise.

In my fourth point, I ask for the host countries' *adherence to a minimum set of rules of a market economy.* Everybody will agree, that competition is beneficial to consumers and to the overall efficiency of a country's economy; I am also convinced, that a free market economy combined with social legislation and social responsibility is finally the best system for the man in the street and the working people.

My last point is, that a multinational company needs an *adequate remuneration for services rendered.* We have to maintain a level of return which will allow us to think and act on a long-term basis. This minimum level of return is in any case only a minor portion compared to the value added and the overall economic benefit to the host country.

Some countries consider foreign know-how necessary but want to get it at the cheapest possible price. They will, I think, be disappointed because everything has its price and companies and investors act and react according to the possible rewards and advantages they gain from their activities and investments over the long run.

Let me return at the end of my reflections to some of Nestlé's basic principles in the discussions with host country governments and to our attitude as economic agent in a foreign country.

We will in the future more than ever be successful not through domination, but through cooperation with the countries in which we are working. Our overall contribution to the economic and social development of the world will also be our contribution to the progress of ideas, rather than to the idea of so-called «progress»!

But cooperation can only be successful if linked with responsibility. I firmly believe that without a responsible attitude and the will to maintain this attitude, nobody has the right to exercise long-term authority and, if you like, power. Governments, institutions, such as universities, and economic agents, such as multinational companies, must be aware of this and act accordingly.

I strongly believe that without overall basic principles and the corresponding attitudes in leadership we will in the long-term not be able to keep the authority, respect, and legitimacy necessary to fulfill our tasks in the world economy.

Aussenwirtschaft, 41. Jahrgang (1986), Heft I, Grüsch: Rüegger, S.47–53

The Importance of Direct Investment for Developing Countries

Adolfo Hegewisch
Vice Minister, Ministry of Commerce
Director General of Foreign Investments, Mexico

This topic is extremely complex and controversial. Therefore, in order to approach it correctly, we need to deal first of all with the general situation of developing countries, then we should speak about the controversial role of direct and indirect foreign investment in the developing world, and we can conclude by discussing future trends and perspectives.

The international economic situation does not present midterm favourable prospects for developing countries making strong efforts to restructure their production sector in order to enter world markets on competitive terms.

In Latin-America, due to the 1984 economic results, several countries have been forced to comply more rigorously with calls for adjustment policies as a result of the urgent need, on the one hand, to renegotiate their external debt and on the other, to reject solutions that meant declaring a moratorium. 1985 thus shows an uneven pattern. Those countries that have adjusted their economies successfully will have less pressure in the near future. Thus, recovery in their gross domestic product is feasible and in addition, inflation will reach more manageable levels. Those countries that deviated from the initial program, however, will have to make an additional adjustment, with corresponding consequences for gross domestic product, investment and unemployment. Nonetheless, it could be expected that in 1985, for the first time since 1980, the inflation rate in Latin-America would be lower than that of the previous year.

Despite the recovery in the North American economy, the expectations of an increase in Latin-American exports, as well as price improvements in most basic goods, have been disappointed. In real terms we can see that exports find growing obstacles in protectionism, in addition to the damage caused by deteriorating terms of trade and present interest rates that are still high. The only element that has lessened the negative effects of the adjustment policy is some countries' ability to decrease their imports, without having a contraction in the GNP as could be expected.

Displacements in international industries and the rearrangement of commercial trends opened gaps in certain sectors for the developing countries, but it cannot be taken for granted that this re-opening is going to occur regularly and progressively.

On the other hand, the situation which the developing countries are experiencing calls for the rational use and allocation of all available resources, in order to accelerate our economic re-activation in the shortest time possible. This policy would aim at overcoming the various effects of the crisis, that, to a certain point, relates to the implementation of a development strategy that did not consider sufficiently its external economic links.

The main economic deficiencies have basically resulted in imbalances of the production and distribution sectors, which in turn, have resulted in a very high vulnerability abroad. This represents an obstacle to achieving sustained growth.

It also means insufficient internal savings to meet the basic needs of a constantly growing population, lack of foreign currency – this is explained, among other reasons, by rigidity in the substitution of internal and external savings –, low competitiveness of domestic products, lack of proper channels for external marketing, acute dependence on imports, protectionist behaviour of developed economies and uneven distribution of development benefits.

So then, external debt – both public and private – has become an adjustment variable of the internal economic evolution and has acted as a compensation for the structural deficiencies of the industrial sector. In most cases, exports of manufactured goods were not the result of a permanent strategy with the aim of penetrating international markets, but rather, resulted from surpluses that the domestic market could not absorb.

We have observed the phenomenon of growing economic inter-relations mainly due to the dynamic growth of communications which make distances shorter and shorter every day. This has caused international economic and political relations to expand and intertwine in such a way that an individual country cannot live in autarchy any longer.

Today, we live in a world where distances are no longer an obstacle to commercial and financial relations and this trend towards internationalization has gone far ahead of limited ideological attitudes which forbid looking beyond their own frontiers.

International trade has grown exponentially in recent years, increasing the interdependence among countries and their respective industrial sectors. Moreover, pressures on international markets for the development of new products and economies of scale have resulted in international corporations of various countries agreeing to diversify their manufacturing operations around the world based on comparative advantages offered by the receiving countries.

As far as direct foreign investment is concerned, before World War I, more than 50 per cent of the world investments were in the primary sector, in other words, in agriculture and raw materials. 20 per cent were in railroads, 15 per cent in manufacturing and 10 per cent in services.

After World War II, there was a dramatic change that put manufacturing as the main investment sector, both in developed and in developing countries. Investment was mainly directed towards developing countries rich in natural resources and with a relatively high per-capita income. This shift towards the manufacturing sector encompassed both developed and developing nations. Investments were made mainly in food, chemicals and capital goods. In the service sector, investments were mainly centered in banks, insurances and, to a lesser degree, tourism, advertising, marketing and distribution. In the extraction sector, investment went basically to the petroleum industry, copper and bauxite.

At present, there is a relocation of investment that comes out of, but goes mainly to, developed countries. It differs from the situation prevailing before World War II where most investments went to the exploitation of raw materials in developing countries.

On the other hand, the importance of international direct investment in the net financial flow to developing countries has gradually declined, giving way to a rapid expansion of international indirect investment through bank loans and credit lines for exports. So, while in the period of 1968-1970 direct investment accounted for 22.1 per cent of the total capital imports of the developing countries, for 1978-1980 this figure dropped down to 13.9 per cent. It is evident that too much was financed via debt and very little through capital contributions.

That is the reason why in developing countries the quantitative participation of direct foreign investment is very limited vis-à-vis indirect investment. In the case of Mexico, the external debt service reaches approximately 12 billion dollars a year. This figure represents roughly 80 per cent of the total direct investment in the country and 45 per cent of our exports.

Without a reasonable amount of fresh capital to absorb the general impact of the world recession, those projects which were financed 100 per cent by external debt started to be in trouble.

International banks, along with many others, made the mistake of not realizing how dangerous this structural defect was. This became evident at the beginning of the world recession.

If international credit societies had acted basically as development banks, that is to say, not only in lending money but also in contributing risk capital to developing countries' priority projects, the crisis these nations are suffering would not have been as severe as it is nowadays.

The increase of indirect foreign investment responded to a great extent to an important trend towards regulating direct foreign investments, as opposed to indirect foreign investments that did not have any regulation at all. These latter investments were not only free of any specific regulation but there were not even the mechanisms indispensable to any control of its inflow and outflow.

This statement could seem unimportant, since structural defects derived from a growing indebtness clearly show a greater damage to our economies than the one generated by the low amount of direct foreign investment.

It has to be mentioned that the distribution of foreign investment flows is not based on moral principles, but on the need to use world resources efficiently. Therefore, risk capital is oriented towards those nations that offer comparative advantages, such as a wide market, infrastructures, abundant raw materials at international prices, political stability and competent labor.

Multinational companies, when evaluating investment projects in developing countries, should, in turn, consider mutual-benefit commitments which are more realistic and coherent with the development strategies implemented by local governments.

Among those instruments and formulas for development finance we believe thorough consideration should be given to development capital contributions by these companies.

In addition, when facing the problems of lack of foreign currency, it would be advisable that subsidiaries should be able to pay their headquarters profits, royalties and other payments with products manufactured by their own plants or by other companies in the country.

Moreover, in order to update the production sector and to generate foreign currency, companies with foreign capital supplying the domestic market should implement in-bond (Maquila) processes for their headquarters or third parties abroad. This would allow them to increase the competitiveness of their products as a first step towards their own exports.

Establishing twin plants is a system that so far has had little development but should be pursued further. In this case, advantage should be taken of two worlds. On the developed side of the border, parts that require high technology should be manufactured; the developing country's side should be dedicated to assembly processes that call for high volumes of labor. With this arrangement, a proper use of the production assets of each nation could be achieved.

An additional method of financing industries in developing countries could be the establishment of risk capital enterprises in joint-ventures between domestic and international banks. Profits from these ventures would be guaranteed, since capital would only be invested in high-feasibility projects.

All the above mentioned instruments respond to the need to see direct foreign investments from a perspective beyond limited concepts such as capital percentages and investment flow amounts. Qualitative factors such as the creation of an exporting plant, efficient import substitution and technology transfer should also be taken into account.

In this context, recent policies on foreign investments show a trend aiming at a balance between foreign participation regulations, the development of such contributions and their channeling to specific sectors and the trend towards a flexible application of these policies.

Traditionally a number of developing countries have kept liberal or open-door policies. However, they have not been able to attract important investments from transnational companies due to several reasons, i.e. small markets or limited natural resources.

Some developing countries that established regulating mechanisms for control purposes in the seventies, encourage direct foreign investments by offering profitable domestic markets, natural resources or other incentives.

Recent trends in these countries show considerable liberalization of their policies towards transnational companies and a flexible application of regulations.

In another group of developing countries, including some socialist countries, present policies show a complete change regarding the restrictive criteria applied to foreign investments in the past. In some countries, liberalization has been enormous, while in some others it has been selective and has been applied to specific sectors and objectives. We could mention as an example more than half of the member countries of COMECON. They have laws whereby their governments are allowed to enter into joint-business agreements with western companies. Cuba and North Korea have also recently opened their doors to such investments.

The juridical framework of direct foreign investments in Latin-America suggests the existence of two different models in most countries of the region. A first model is one referring to the Andean group and the Dominican Republic. This is a regime of compulsory performance formally oriented towards income and operational control of foreign investments. The second model has as its goal the attraction of and the creation of proper conditions for foreign capital inflow and performance.

Concerning the traditional policy of the Latin-American nations there has been a complete turn-round in the attitude that rejected international arbitration as a way of settling matters related directly to foreign investors, with the creation of the Overseas Private International Corporation (OPIC). To date, this agency has signed agreements with several Latin-American countries and in most cases, it grants the possibility of settling matters via international arbitration should American multinational companies be involved. There is no doubt that this step represents a more flexible position regarding direct foreign investments.

As far as the previous permit is concerned, it is a compulsory requirement of the Andean Countries and the ALADI. This permit should be issued by an authority with specific power for these matters. In other countries, even though the authorization is requested formally, it is denied only in exceptional cases.

On an analysis of the evolution of treatment of foreign capital, it is evident that at present 13 nations of this area have specific regulations governing foreign investments. All these nations, with the exception of the Dominican Republic and Nicaragua belong to the ALADI. This means that in Central-America and the Caribbean the trend to regulate such investments organically has not been established, but rather, there is some encouragement for this foreign capital inflow. It has even reached the point where there is even some competition among these nations to offer the biggest incentives to attract these investments.

To conclude, there is an international agreement towards more flexible regulations on foreign investments, together with more possibilities of incentives and guarantees. It could be said that this trend answers profound changes in the domestic socio-economic conditions, most particularly, to the rhythm and characteristics of the industrialization process and to the transformations implemented in world production structures.

Finally, I would not like to finish without saying that my country is passing through dark and difficult days. Nonetheless, we believe that it is in hard times like these that great nations are formed. There is light at the end of the tunnel for the country, like Mexico, that fights for itself. We shall fight on all fronts. We shall not give up in our fight against inflation; we shall keep our policy of realistic prices, less subsidies, less deficit, openings to foreign trade, and we shall continue promoting direct foreign investment that will help the development of Mexico, and under your trust, it will share in the benefits of a promising future.

Part II

Promotion of Foreign Private Investment by the International Finance Corporation (IFC)

Aussenwirtschaft, 41. Jahrgang (1986), Heft I, Grüsch: Rüegger, S.57–70

Investing for Development in a Changing World

F. Javier Alejo
Vice President, International Finance Corporation (IFC)

The aim of this paper is not to recite the liturgy of IFC's investment policies.[1] Rather, I want to focus on the climate for private investment in LDCs, to consider some of the problems that are arising in the Third World, and to show how IFC is adapting to this changing world. Our views of development evolve; so does our role. I felt therefore that it would be more appropriate to examine how we view the world economy, the problems of developing countries, how our policies are being molded and to discuss the basis of these policies without being restricted by a formal recitation of rules and regulations. There is something, however, that never changes in IFC: our conviction of the importance of mobilizing the enormous potential hidden among entrepreneurs in developing countries.

Interdependence in a Changing World

It has recently become almost a truism to say that we live in an interdependent and changing world. There is perhaps no better way to illustrate the growing interdependence of the world economy than by the following assertion: a combination of unstable oil prices, abnormally high interest rates, developing countries' balance of payments deficits, large-scale medium-term loans from the private banking system and non-coordinated deflationary and reflationary macroeconomic policies in OECD countries have led to a situation in which intolerable economic pressures in distant countries can threaten the savings or livelihood of the citizen of an American small town or a European village.[2]

Several determinants have brought about this intensification of interdependence. All of them continue to shape and reshape the «world

---

[1] For this see Appendix

[2] M. Stewart, *The Age of Interdependence,* the MIT Press, Cambridge, Mass., 1984, p. 24.

economy». The main driving force in the making of our interdependent economy was the extraordinary expansion of world trade during the sixties and the seventies when world trade grew much faster than world output. Between 1965 and 1978 the exports of developed market economies grew about 80 percent faster than their industrial production. Foreign trade grew as a proportion of GDP of all industrial economies. The post-war period had created a basically free trade environment among industrialized nations, even though the liberalization process lost momentum at the end of the seventies and the deep recession that followed triggered very dangerous protectionist moves towards developing countries' manufacturing exports. Some additional factors for the expansion of trade were the economic modernization and undervalued currencies of Germany and Japan, the European Communities and the emergence and growth of multinational corporations. The main implication of the grand expansion of international trade was that the level of output and employment of individual countries is now considerably more dependent than it used to be on decisions made by consumers, businesses and goverments in other countries.

The second major determinant of a growing interdependence was two-fold: the financial explosion of borrowing and lending across the globe in the middle and late 1970s and the increasing mobility of short-term capital. During 1975-82 the developing countries ran deficits on current accounts of 60 billion dollars a year, the bulk of which was financed by the private international banking community. A combination of historically high real interest rates in 1983-84, wide-spread and deep recession in all OECD countries, protectionist measures in those countries, and abnormally low prices for all raw materials and commodities produced a massive external shock for the economies of many developing countries. In some cases, this shock was such that all the gains in per capita income made by earlier efforts were lost. Many developing countries appear, under these conditions, incapable of both reassuming growth and of servicing their external debts.

The emergence of large surpluses in the hands of many OPEC members (now declining), the adoption of the new floating exchange rate system plus the dismantling of capital transfer barriers in most OECD countries caused an explosion in the eurocurrency markets which had been developing since the late 1950s and early 1960s. By 1984 the amount of eurocurrency loans had reached almost 2 trillion dollars (including interbank transactions). The implication of this is that very large sums of money can be switched very quickly from the one country or currency to another in response to actual or anticipated changes in interest rates, exchange rates or economic conditions generally. The result, as huge amounts of a particular currency are bought or sold, can be big changes in exchange rates in very short time, as well as gains or losses in foreign exchange reserves, which can be very large in relation to the initial stock. The sheer dimension of this phenomenon allows us to imagine the intensity of its effects on the economies and standards of living of developing countries.

That is why interdependence (or at least one side of it) has for long been an obvious fact of life for most developing countries, just as nowadays it is becoming obvious for almost everybody. The immediate and obvious consequence is that nobody can enjoy the luxury of ignoring the repercussions of his own decisions on others. Nor can others' reactions and their impact upon one's own economy be ignored.

This unstable and complex situation has resulted from many years of changes, which have been inexorable, even unavoidable. The weakest side is the developing countries. They lack the basic and necessary instruments, and room for maneuver, to cope with the vagaries of the international economy and the shocks such vagaries impose on them. It is now crystal clear that the single most important threat to peace and stability is the crisis which confronts many developing countries.

Four major external factors pose the main threat: the level and mechanics of debt service, the abnormally high interest rates, the growing protectionism in industrialized countries and the lack of sufficient additional finance to keep LDC economies growing at least minimally.

Changing Patterns in Financial Flows to LCDs

During the last two decades there have been two major shifts in the flow of international capital to LDCs: from equity to debt and from official to private finance.[1] Prior to the Second World War, equity finance and bond issues in international capital markets were the dominant form of development finance but war reparations and the emergence of the U.S. as the main creditor nation brought government borrowing and lending into the picture during the interwar period. After the Second World War and until 1960, Official Development Assistance (ODA) and private direct foreign investment represented the bulk of international capital flow to developing countries, with ODA contributing more than 50%. By 1970 commercial

[1] IBRD, *World Development Report, 1985,* Oxford University Press, 1985, pp. 18 – 20.

bank lending was contributing almost as much as equity private investment, ODA's contribution was less than 50 %. By 1980 the latter represented only 40% and commercial international banks had outpaced private direct investment. By 1983 the two taken together were the single most important factor, with almost 45%, but equity investment alone contributed less than 10%.

The more advanced developing countries obviously obtained the bulk of commercial capital, but even in the low income countries the share of private flows increased. The weight of debt-creating foreign capital gained particular prominence during the 1970s. For all developing countries, receipts of medium- and long-term loans averaged 4.4% of GNP over the decade, reaching 5.7% in 1979. These funds financed between 10 and 21 percent of gross domestic investment in that period, with large variations among countries.

Although private direct investment continued to increase in nominal terms during the 1970s, its share in total external finance declined from 20 percent in 1970 to less than 9 percent in 1983. Export credits grew fast during the 1970s but have declined sharply in recent years. So the main factor by far was lending by commercial banks. The result of this process is that by the end of 1984 the total external liabilities of LDCs had reached almost 900 billion dollars. An additional change was in the direction of higher interest rates, shorter maturities, and a larger share of floating rate debt, which rose from 16 percent in 1974 to 43 percent in 1983. Average maturities of public debts fell from 20.4 years in 1970 to 14.2 years in 1982, and grace periods from 5.5 years to 3.9 years. Interest on long-term loans to public borrowers grew from 7.0 percent in 1974-76 to 10.5 percent in 1980-82.

As a result of this process, debt service ratios jumped from 14.7 percent in 1970 to 20.5 percent in 1982 as an average for all LDCs. In the case of the middle-income oil exporters, debt service ratios increased from 11.0 percent in 1974 to 28.1 percent in 1984, with interest payments being almost 4 percent of GDP of those countries in 1984.

In the last 2 to 3 years, almost all over-indebted countries have undergone massive and sizable adjustments of their economies, under the guidance of the IMF. However, they are still suffering from a protracted and very dangerous recession, in many cases still combined with high inflation. One of the main causes is a lack of sufficiently balanced and appropriate finance. There has been a dramatic decline in the volume of international finance accruing to developing countries. The decline has taken place in all forms of financing: official funds, multilateral lending, commercial lending, direct private investment and portfolio private investment. The scarcity has been even sharper when it comes to financing long-term economic growth. This is why, I assume, Secretary Baker made his enlightened plea to the international financial community during the annual meetings of IBRD/IMF in Seoul, Korea, to increase the volume and quality of lending and transfer of resources to the troubled developing countries. The need for a balanced approach is self-evident since no single source of finance will solve the problem: everyone will have to contribute if we want to find a solution.

It is also true that the main part of any solution lies with the troubled developing countries themselves. The possibility of turning their present condition around will certainly depend upon their ability to eliminate price distortions, increase and mobilize domestic savings, reduce public deficits, and open up their economies to external competition, under reasonable levels and efficient systems of protection. But these efforts, if undertaken, will almost certainly be frustrated if they are not properly and sufficiently financed, given the structural scarcity of capital which is characteristic of those economies. A minimum continuous long-term net flow of foreign resources equivalent to 1.0–3.0 percent of LDCs' GDP is indispensable. It must also be provided on a long-term basis and at reasonable interest rates.

As for the needed structural changes, the troubled developing countries can find a good example to examine and reflect upon in the experience of those countries — notably Korea, Malaysia, Singapore, Thailand and Taiwan — which managed to industrialize their economies without getting indebted beyond their capacity to repay on reasonable terms. The common features of their experience are that they incurred minimal distortions of price structures, promoted exports, promoted high levels of domestic savings, indulged only in manageable fiscal deficits and created an institutional and economic environment which encouraged private investment, domestic and foreign. They opened up their domestic economies gradually along with the process of their maturing.

When it comes to financial flows, bilateral and multilateral ODA will no doubt have to cope with most of the needs of the least developed countries. In the case of the maturing and already mature LDCs' economies, private flows will have to play a dominant role, even though some amount of multilateral development banks' assistance will continue to be needed. Here is where the International Finance Corporation comes into the picture.

The IFC and the Role of the Private Sector

There is no doubt that private financial flows, certainly in the case of equity investment, are determined by profit opportunities and the perception of risks. They also depend upon the struggle to control or enlarge market shares, raw material sources or the improvement of cost structures.

The international economic situation has improved significantly in the past year, but the improvement has been uneven and has benefited only a very small number of LDCs.

In the industrialized countries, gross domestic product grew by 4.9 percent last year, the best performance since 1979. Among developing countries, GDP grew by 5.0 percent, fuelled by an export growth of almost 11 percent.

While that may sound good across the board, a closer look at the details shows just how uneven economic performance has been in the developing world. In Asia, for example, GDP grew by 8.7 percent (9.0 percent in East Asia) while in Africa growth was only 0.8 percent and in Latin America it was 3.1 percent.

Generally, the middle-income countries that did not indebt themselves heavily grew steadily, but the heavily indebted countries, barring a few exceptions, have yet to subdue inflation. Moreover, their external accounts are beginning to show signs of renewed deterioration.

There is no doubt that the debt crisis has caused severe problems, not the least of which has been a drying up of the flow of external capital into developing countries. During the 1983 – 84 period, for example, only $ 33 billion of net new private lending flowed to developing countries, compared to a net flow of $ 132 billion during 1981 and 1982. Net direct investment declined from an average of $ 11.6 billion per year in 1979 – 82 to $ 9 billion in 1984.

There are other clouds on the horizon too. One is a possible slowdown of growth in the developing countries. Among OECD countries, gross domestic product growth fell from about 7 percent in the first half of 1984 to an estimated 3 percent in the first half of 1985. A second concern is the continued abnormally low level of prices for primary commodities.

So we have a fairly serious economic situation as a backdrop to our consideration of investment in the developing world. And it is not a situation that will necessarily respond to short-term or «bandaid» solutions.

So, how do we at IFC view the situation of the private sector in developing countries within this context?

At the present time, the private investment climate is best in middle income countries that did not contract over-powering debt. Most of these countries are in Asia and include such open, export-oriented economies as Korea, Malaysia and Thailand. But other countries favourable for private investment also include less open countries such as Colombia, India and Pakistan and a few oil exporters like Cameroon and Indonesia. All of these countries have followed relatively conservative demand management policies and have been quick to curtail government expenditure when necessary. Private business in these countries has shared in the problems related to high interest rates and world-wide recession, but the impact has been relatively mild and growth rebounded in 1984.

At the other extreme are those countries suffering both from high debt and a heavy reliance on commodity exports. In Peru, for example, private investment in 1984 was half what it was in 1980. In Zambia total investment has fallen by about 40 percent in that same four year period.

Zambia, in fact, is a sad example of the debt/commodity syndrome, and the country has fallen so deeply into an economic sinkhole that international lending agencies, major donors and local bankers say it is incapable of borrowing or producing its way out. As a Zambian banker told the *Washington Post* recently, «rescheduling our debts and borrowing more money will give us some breathing space, but it will merely put off the evil day. Frankly, we cannot generate enough money to pay the debts and buy the imports that keep the country going».

Zambia's problems are complex, but at the heart of them is the fact that the country depended on the price of copper for 90 percent of its export earnings and, in 1975, the price of copper collapsed and never recovered. Today, copper prices are still 60 percent lower than they were 10 years ago. The country has virtually no foreign exchange and is totally dependent on international sources of money for it to keep going at all. At the present moment, debt service drains away 82 percent of new loans coming into the country and interest payments on the country's debt would eat up 40 percent of the country's export earnings if Zambia met these payments – which it does not. No wonder, you say, that investment in Zambia is down 40 percent.

Among debtor countries with more diversified exports, the situation is healthier, but not exactly euphoric. Mexico, with exports up and its foreign debt restructured, resumed moderate growth last year, but inflation rebounded and the Peso became more unstable. Brazil's growth is also on the move again, and dramatic increases in exports in both 1983 and 1984 have helped alleviate the debt burden.

Most of the small, low-income countries rely heavily on agriculture and mining. Thus, they are particularly susceptible to climatic vagaries and the unpredictable movements of the international commodity markets. While some of these countries have made strenuous and effective efforts to stabilize their economies, others are only just starting to come to grips with their problems. In these countries, demand is slack, financial resources are scarce and private investment is very low. Both Kenya and the Ivory Coast are cases in point.

Private sector development in this uneven and difficult environment is actually receiving increasingly favorable attention from the governments concerned, as well as from international financial institutions. We are seeing liberalization of controls on prices, private investment and foreign trade. Foreign investment is being welcomed, particularly for small and medium-sized projects, and there are even cases where state-owned enterprises are being transferred to private operation.

It is ironic that the private sector is regaining favor just at the time when so many private firms in these countries have been weakened by the events of the past few years. But it is true, however, that these are countries in which a single well planned private investment can turn around the whole balance of payments picture of the country. That is, for example, the case of the investments we are arranging for Trinidad-Tobago.

As we look to the future, then, we must hope that the governments of developing countries will strive to develop an atmosphere in which market forces and private enterprise are given more encouragement. They must also encourage an increasing share for equity investment in the flow of capital. How can we achieve this? The IFC provides advice in this respect when so requested.

Obviously the two are connected. Why was the balance of capital flows in the 1970s distorted in favor of commercial bank lending and against equity investment? Partly because of the pressure on the banks to lend the money that arose from the oil surpluses that were in effect then. But it lies also in the attitudes of many developing country governments who were suspicious of foreign investment and the role of multinational corporations. This is now changing. In India, for example, where there has long been an aversion to investment from abroad, there is a strong trend towards reconsiderating this attitude. Mr. Rajiv Gandhi is encouraging this development. And of course, China is now opening to foreign investment to a degree that would have been unthinkable 10 years ago.

An important change has also taken place among the international institutions concerned with development. The World Bank, for example, is giving much more emphasis to private sector development by encouraging governments to create a policy environment in which the private sector can thrive, and by providing finance which supports private investment.

But the institution within the World Bank Family that is particularly devoted to increasing the role of the private sector in development is the one I represent: IFC. IFC's mission is development through private enterprise. We do not lend to governments, we invest in companies. We are precluded by our charter from accepting a government guarantee on any loan or equity investment we make.

We act as a catalyst. We are always a minority participant in any venture, usually subscribing 15 to 20 percent (25% maximum) in the form of loans and equity.

Our financial role may not be large, but our key role is bringing others together to invest with us, and by working with all concerned, we often make things happen that would not otherwise happen. In fact, IFC is the largest source of direct project financing for private investment in the developing world. To date, we have been involved with more than 2,000 companies and financial institutions in supporting 850 business ventures in over 80 countries.

We are not here to do what the private sector can do for itself, but this means that we are challenged to take on risks that make others hesitate. Sometimes there are risks which we believe we are well equipped to help others carry. For example, foreign investors sometimes hesitate because they see a political risk or a country risk or perhaps they see a problem in securing foreign exchange to finance operations or service debts. The presence of IFC, a member of the World Bank Family, in a venture can provide reassurance and reduce the perceived risk. In other cases, IFC's careful planning and analysis can actually reduce the degree of risk.

Although we undertake risky projects, we are still governed, like any other investor, by profit considerations. Some people argue that our role as a development institution must, by definition, conflict with the need to make a profit. We strongly disagree. We believe that it is only through profitable investments that we contribute to development, because only profitable investments enlarge the wealth and resources of the host country. And from a purely selfish point of view, we have to make a profit to sustain ourselves. Fortunately, we have done so consistently year after year, although like any other investor, we have lost money on some of our individual ventures.

Now, IFC's role is expanding and changing. Last year, our board decided to double our capital to 1,300 million dollars. With this broader resource base we plan to double our investments over the coming five years, investing some $4.5 billion for our own account and a further $3 billion for the account of banks to whom we expect to sell participation in our projects.

If all goes well, these investments will be our contribution to projects that will total close to $30 billion.

We intend to play a more aggressive role in the development process in the future, and this will mean not only more and larger investments but also some quite new activities. For this purpose we are continuously adding new financial services and instruments to comply with changing project needs. That is why we have put forward floating rate financing, swaps, partial guarantees, and all forms of quasi-equity financing.

We will be looking for ways to expand the industrial sectors in which we operate, and for ways in which we can help to introduce technologies which can benefit the economies of the developing world.

We will be strengthening our capacity for providing advice and technical assistance to governments on subjects such as legislation governing foreign investment, development of their country's capital markets and improvement of their overall business environment.

We will be enlarging our activities in the development of financial institutions and capital markets. This is an area where IFC has played an important and indeed unique role. We have helped countries establish stock markets and securities markets. We have helped to establish funds used to channel portfolio investments in some countries. We have created venture capital companies and leasing companies. We have set up housing finance and savings institutions. We see growing potential for this kind of activity.

We are increasingly active in the restructuring of existing enterprises as an alternative to setting up new ventures. We see ourselves becoming increasingly involved in restructuring enterprises currently owned by governments that wish to turn them over to private enterprise. We have already been asked by a number of governments to become involved in this process.

Sub-Saharan Africa will receive an increasing amount of our attention. We are planning to set up, in cooperation with other international organizations, a special African project development facility that will undertake appraisal and design work for private sector projects. We also hope to set up a facility to provide skilled manpower on contract. This will help solve one of the main problems for investment in Africa – the shortage of skilled human resources.

We are going to be much more flexible in dealing with moderate sized investments. Potential partners have often expressed the view that we are only interested in big projects. This is not so. We think we can be equally helpful to smaller enterprises, and can be particularly helpful if we are called in at an early stage in the preparation of a project.

We are also going to work hard to dispel the view – I like to think of it as a misconception – that IFC is slow, inflexible and bureaucratic. «The mills of God grind slowly, yet they grind exceeding small», or in other words, what sometimes seems to be bureaucratic lethargy is really the process of careful analysis that can protect the investor in the long run. Still, we recognize that we sometimes do not act in accordance with the urgency of the market place. We intend to improve. More and more people are joining IFC from the corporate and business world. They are bringing a different perspective to our work, and making the rest of us look at our role more objectively. We talk about the measure of the market place – we intend to listen to our own words.

Were you to ask me to choose an adjective that describes IFC today, I would probably come up with something like *«thorough.»* If you were to ask me to come with the adjective I would like you to use to describe IFC tomorrow, I would choose *«aggressive.»* We have some way to go before I can be satisfied that we have made that transition successfully but we are making progress. Perhaps today I have given evidence that we are moving in the right direction.

Appendix

International Finance Corporation

The International Finance Corporation (IFC), an affiliate of the World Bank, was established in 1956 to promote private investment in developing countries by encouraging the flow of domestic and foreign capital into productive private enterprise.

Capital Resources

IFC's capital, subscribed by 126 member countries, was approximately $544 million as of June 30, 1984. The resources available to IFC are supported by accumulated earnings of $230 million, by repayments and by sales to others of IFC investments. The Corporation can also borrow for use in its lending operations up to four times the amount of its unimpaired subscribed capital and accumulated earnings – that is, about $3,100 million.

In June 1984, IFC's Board of Directors approved a resolution for a $650 million increase in IFC's capital. If agreed upon by the member countries, IFC's authorized capital will increase to $1.3 billion. This increase will permit the Corporation to accelerate its investment program and it expects, over the next five years, to invest about $7.4 billion in more than 400 projects with total project costs of approximately $30 billion.

Other Resources

In addition to its funds, IFC has other resources available to local and foreign entrepreneurs, sponsors, technical partners, and other investors associated with a project. The Corporation's international staff – in which 68 countries are represented – has accumulated much financial, legal and technical expertise relevant to investment opportunities and to the anticipation and solution of investment problems in the developing world. IFC can also draw on the World Bank's wide experience, as well as on its own contacts with financial institutions and development agencies.

Conditions and Forms of Investment

1. Eligible Areas

All developing member countries.

2. Type of Business

Most types of productive private enterprise. IFC is prepared to support «mixed» enterprises, i.e., joint ventures between private enterprise and government. Each case is examined in the light of such factors as the extent of Government ownership and control, the nature of the enterprise, efficiency of management and the possibility of increasing the extent of private ownership in the future.

3. Investment Criteria

Venture must benefit economy of host country.
Venture must hold prospect of profit.
Sufficient private capital cannot be obtained on reasonable terms.
Host government does not object to proposed investment.
Local investors should be able to participate in the venture, at the outset or later.

4. Forms of IFC financing

(a) IFC investments for its own account generally are no more than 25 percent of the project cost and it normally provides between $1 million and $50 million. However, it can also raise substantial funds in addition to its own investment for larger projects. It may invest less than its normal $1 million lower limit, especially in ventures in the smaller and least developed countries, pilot operations and promotional companies.

(b) IFC financing may be in the form of a long-term loan or a share subsription, or a combination of both.

(c) The type of IFC investment, the investment mix and the investment terms will vary from case to case depending upon the circumstances involved, the risk entailed and the prospective return. IFC follows a flexible policy, being prepared within the limits of its investment criteria to do whatever needs to be done to get a sound enterprise moving.

(d) The loan portions of IFC investments normally run for a term of seven to 12 years and are usually amortized by semi-annual or quarterly payments after a suitable period of grace. Loans are normally denominated in US dollars, but they may be expressed in other currencies.
A commitment fee at the rate of 1 percent per year is payable on the undisbursed portion of a loan.
Interest rates on loans vary according to the circumstances of particular transactions.

(e) Investments in share capital are normally denominated in local currency.

(f) IFC considers important the extent of the sponsor's participation in the share capital of an enterprise. Where its investment takes the form of equity, IFC will not normally provide more than 25 percent of the share capital of the venture, preferring it to be well under that figure. Only rarely is IFC willing to be the largest single shareholder in an enterprise.

(g) IFC can provide financing through standby or underwriting arrangements in support of public offerings or private placements of shares, debentures and other corporate securities. It is prepared to act as sole underwriter or as a member of an underwriting group, but does not itself engage in the direct sale of securities to the general public.

(h) IFC will make no investment unless appropriate arrangements exist for the repatriation of its investment and the earnings thereon.

(i) IFC neither requires nor accepts government guarantees of repayment on its investments.

5. Use of IFC Funds

May be used for expenditures in any of the 148 countries belonging to The World Bank or in Switzerland.

May be used for foreign or local expenditures, to acquire assets or for working capital.

6. Management

IFC expects its investment partners to provide management, and does not itself assume management responsibilities. IFC does not generally accept representation on the board of directors of a business enterprise in which it invests, although it may do so if a particular purpose is to be served thereby. Only in exceptional circumstances will IFC exercise its voting rights as a shareholder.

7. Project Supervision

IFC expects to consult periodically with management, to send field missions to visit the enterprise and to receive regular quarterly progress reports together with information on factors materially affecting or likely to affect an enterprise in which it has invested. It also requires annual financial statements audited by independent public accountants.

Aussenwirtschaft, 41. Jahrgang (1986), Heft I, Grüsch: Rüegger, S.71–80

Case Studies: IFC Projects

Dr. Hans Pollan
Special Representative in Europe
International Finance Corporation, London

The typical IFC project is usually of a size with a total investment cost including permanent working capital, of about $20–50 million. The domestic partners, preferably a private company, contribute anywhere between 25% and over 50% of the equity capital; the foreign partner, who also brings in technical expertise, about 25% to 40%; and IFC anywhere between 10 and 20%. The debt: equity ratio that we look for is usually conservative, but adjusted to the nature of the business, that varies anywhere between 1:1, most conservatively, to, in some instances, 2½ – 3:1.

Credit financing is basically provided both from domestic and foreign sources. At times a domestic development bank disposing of a credit line from institutions like the European Investment Bank or the World Bank, provides a foreign exchange credit facility. And there is IFC itself often in association with banks which have entered a syndication agreement with IFC which becomes the lender of record vis-à-vis the ultimate client.

India

One typical recent transaction, in fact denominated in Swiss Francs, was an IFC loan of nearly $16 million to Bajaj Tempo Limited in India for the consolidation and the doubling of the firm's production capacity to 30,000 light commercial vehicles by the end of 1988. The total project cost is estimated at slightly over $50 million. India is already the second largest producer of commercial vehicles in Asia after Japan. Nevertheless, vehicle density in India is quite low and expansion prospects are excellent. The industry is currently undergoing a major modernisation following the recent liberalisation of the Indian Government's licensing policy and the introduction of modern, fuel-efficient vehicle technology. Several other firms are also expanding, and also in the ancillary industry.

Bajaj, established in 1958, is the leading Indian light vehicle producer. 52% of the shares are held by two Indian family groups, 26% by Daimler-Benz, and the rest by the Indian general public. Bajaj approached IFC for a loan to provide about 85% of the project's foreign exchange financing. The company saw this also as an opportunity to introduce itself to the international commercial banks through their participation in IFC's loans. In the end one American and one British bank participated. The balance of financing was provided by Indian term financing institutions and internal cash generation.

Yugoslavia

Most of IFC's projects are not in the high-technology area; we are in the cement business, in milling, in chemicals and fertilisers, in vehicles, also textiles, cellulose and agri-business.

On the other hand, the IFC has shown imagination together with its clients in setting up projects which are particularly adjusted to developmental needs in a particular country or region, and which have not only involved the straightforward pattern, but some which are quite new. Let me, by way of an example, give you the outline of two transactions for which we claim, with some pride, a considerable amount of credit.

In Yugoslavia IFC has traditionally financed individual, rather large size industrial investments. They are to be found in practically all the republics, but given the nature of development of the country, more concentrated in Croatia and Slovenia. Among them are TAM, a joint venture with Humboldt-Deutz, Belisce Papira, a joint venture with Voest, Austria. However, under the stabilisation measures which Yugoslavia has had to go through since 1980 in view of its huge foreign debt, the start up and creation of fresh large projects seemed inadvisable. At the same time the country is under pressure to increase its exports in order to adjust its balance of payments deficit. However, enterprises which are export-oriented and which are seeking or already have a market, were, for the same reason, in difficulty in obtaining sufficient foreign exchange financing to modernise and expand their own production facilities.

We saw an opportunity. What IFC was looking for were the industrial exporters in Yugoslavia which, from a business point of view, had intrinsic advantages for exporting. These were usually not new «green field» industrial projects. We were trying to identify modest expansion schemes or de-bottlenecking schemes, which, when taken care of, would lead to increased exports. We focused on enterprises which already had an export performance so that there was a proven record on which to build. The result of this work is evidenced in several transactions which we had been doing since 1983 in cooperation with the Ljubljanska Banka in Slovenia; the Jugobanka and a further one are currently under consideration with Vojvodjanska Banka. The pattern is more or less the same. We identified quite a number, in the case of Ljubljanska Banka 48, of operating divisions of various enterprises that had good prospects for increasing exports. The total investment cost was about $90 million. We financed the foreign exchange portion of about $32 million. As you can see from the number of projects individually, they are relatively small deals packaged into a global loan from IFC to Ljubljanska Banka.

The key element of the transaction from our point of view was that our financial and engineering people looked directly at each enterprise in the field and got a «hands on» view of the business capabilities and proposals of these enterprises. Ljubljanska Banka, at the same time as being extremely helpful in the whole process, was rather happy to have this experience together with us. In fact some of the appraisal techniques that we applied, including computerisation of the process, is now in place. What Ljubljanska Banka had learned is also being shared out to other Yugoslav financing institutions with which we are forming a similar type of transaction. In essence the IFC team was helpful to the Yugoslavs in helping «to separate the sheep from the goats», and in some cases making specific recommendations for improved project structuring for some of the sub-projects. The operation was by definition manpower intensive, but it was reasonably sure that this guaranteed a high economic pay off for Yugoslavia. In fact we already have some experience as a result of the first Ljubljanska Banka package done in 1983. We have seen that the net foreign exchange earnings before completion of the 48 projects improved by $23 million per annum, and if things now go as we expect them to, these projects should have a pay off in net foreign exchange at terms of one year.

At the same time there was an important side benefit to the Yugoslavs, a benefit which was also of interest to others. We were able to interest financing institutions in Switzerland, in Germany and in Austria in participating in our loans to Ljubljanska Banka and other similar Yugoslav packages. Why would commercial banks among them be interested at a time when their exposure to Yugoslavia was already very high, when they had practically no flexibility for fresh lending? In the end the interest of the financing institutions outside Yugoslavia was influenced as we saw it by the status of the then on-going commercial bank debt rescheduling discussions which were concluded last April/May; the presence of important local German or Swiss firms among the possible equipment supply contractors for the sub-projects; thirdly, the presence of IFC for its umbrella function; and finally, the quality of the other participating banks in the syndicate. To the Yugoslav financial institutions this meant a sort of reintroduction to the commercial term financial markets outside the country. It is too early to say whether our approach in Yugoslavia could be applied to other countries which are undergoing a stabilisation programme, which have a debt problem and which have a modicum of export industries. The concept is certainly valid and our experience gained in these Yugoslav transactions will certainly be in our mind when we might consider situations of this type elsewhere.

Central America

Now to Central America. While this is an account of the emergence of BLADEX, Banco Latinoamericano de Exportaciones S.A., as an important regional Latin American export bank, it is also an account of how IFC changes policies and approaches to meet new conditions. In this case the challenge was to restore to health a unique Latin American financial institution which has suffered as a consequence of the Latin American debt crisis.

BLADEX's problem was a massive withdrawal of deposits by the international commercial banks – over $300 million dollars between mid-1982 and the end of 1984 – despite a sound portfolio and good earnings. The solution – a $50 million five-year floating rate note sold in the Euromarkets – was structured, organized and successfully executed by IFC. The solution was designed to have maximum impact in restoring the investor's confidence in BLADEX. This transaction was unique in that it was the first new money raised in the international capital markets for any Latin American entity since the debt crisis. It was also the first time IFC had lead managed a Eurodollar bond issue.

In 1970, Robert McNamara, as President of both the World Bank and IFC, became aware that one of the World Bank Group's development mandates was becoming increasingly important, but still was inadequately addressed: the development of domestic financial markets and the financial institutions that made them work. This was related to the problem of how to wean away the expanding semi-industrial countries from official aid financing from the World Bank and IFC by maximizing domestic savings mobilization and increasing the efficiency of its allocation. Part of this effort was naturally directed to improving access on favorable terms to the international banking and capital markets. This led to the formation of a new department in IFC called the Capital Markets Department. Further, not until the Latin American debt crises of the early 80s was it understood that developing countries could not be «graduated» from offical aid financing, in the face of worsening terms of trade and higher interest costs, if the only financing alternatives were even more dependence on direct investment and the already substantially over-exposed commercial banks.

The development of BLADEX must be read in the context of the above background.

BLADEX was originally conceived in the mid-1970s as a regional export financing mechanism to finance «non-traditional» exports and imports, as well as a means of providing essential pre-export and post-export financing from the region and between countries within the region.

The idea, born in the region, led to an approach to IFC which suggested that, if the ownership structure was private sector oriented, and if the institutional mechanism proposed had the configuration of a private sector managed financing institution, the project's potentially important contribution to the region's capital market development could be effectively highlighted.

Subsequently BLADEX's regional plannings group together with IFC came up with a broad design and plan for BLADEX giving it a capitalization structure which was predominately Latin American, and was also predominately private sector; the legal structure of a private commercial bank specializing in export finance and; finally, Articles of Association, a Board of Directors and a management structure, and a Policy Statement, which ensured that, within the general context of financing «non-traditional» exports from and within Latin America, it would have the flexibility of a profit making institution.

There were many new industrial and agricultural goods being produced in Latin America which were «small order» type export transactions of which many were within the region rather than to the U.S. or Europe. These were hard for the international banks to handle, essentially geared as they were to large transactions in uncomplicated staple goods being exported from the region. These transactions, thus, were left largely to the local commerical banks to handle if they could. Such transactions – smaller amounts down to the tens of thousands of dollars – were, thus, deemed as non-traditional exports. It was here that the scope was seen for maximizing development for Latin American exports. The «financing gap» (to use a typical IFC term used in defining the need for its services) was to provide additional funds at fair terms and on a dependable basis to meet the forecasted need to finance some $5–10 billion of annual exports of this nature. «Rolled-over» three times a year on average meant a need for constant availability of some $1½ to $3 billion. A «market leading» institution providing some 50% of the initial financing would help attract others and, thus, ultimately, by later providing only 10% or about $1 billion, would become a catalyst in encouraging the balance to become available from the larger pool of $100 billion financing traditional Latin American exports.

The question then in developing the BLADEX concept was how to implement it on a financially viable basis. The new plan included two significant changes. The first was to «wholesale» the export finance credits through Latin American commercial banks. The procedure was that they would have to be shareholders of BLADEX to qualify. The local banks would originate the transactions, handle the paper work, and hold the collateral and operate within overall credit criteria and financial limits approved by BLADEX. BLADEX would also have to be given specific details of each export transaction as appropriate. On repayment of each transaction BLADEX would be reimbursed its advances. This enabled the local commercial bank to obtain export funding often not previously available in foreign exchange. At the same time they would relieve BLADEX of the high cost of handling individual small transactions.

In addition the inclusion of international banks as shareholders was considered useful where it was thought that, as BLADEX's business would not be directly competitive with the international banks they would become willing lenders to BLADEX as a form of a second tier wholesale financing for a type of export which they would not necessarily wish to engage in directly.

BLADEX was incorporated in Panama in 1977. Its shareholding capital was divided into three classes; one for Latin American central banks; another limited to Latin American commercial banks which wished to participate as BLADEX borrowers (but could only do so if the countries had a shareholder in the Class «A» group) and to international institutions. IFC was the only international institutional shareholder and is the largest single shareholder with 7.3% of the total equity. A third was reserved for non-Latin American commercial banks and international institutions.

BLADEX's business developed from its first years through 1982 – the beginning of the debt crisis. Its rise from an idea in the mid-1970s to a significant force in Latin American «non-traditional» exports was fast, impressive, and, as demonstrated by its performance during the years of «pause» beginning in mid-1982, based on prudent banking principles.

Starting with paid-in capital of $24.7 million, by December 31, 1982 its capital had reached $52 million, which was leveraged by deposits and borrowings amounting to $677 million, and total assets were about $734 million.

Importantly, BLADEX's export financing business expanded from a total outstanding of $97 million to 13 countries at December 31, 1979 to $480 million to 19 countries at December 31, 1982. Total loans granted in this period were $2,850 million and involved 3,850 separate transactions.

The Latin American debt crisis began to affect BLADEX during 1982. During the second half of 1982, BLADEX suffered a decline in commercial bank funding of $120 million. Calendar 1983 showed a further decline of deposits and other loans of almost $180 million net; 1983 also saw a significant decline in the term of deposits as well as an increase in delinquencies, although the latter were still low.

1984 showed some improvement in total deposits and loans to BLADEX. However, the quality declined as the overall debt crisis continued. Term loans declined a further $28 million net and the term of deposits continued to shorten, while international Certificate of Deposits and loans remained essentially flat. In short, since the beginning of the debt crisis in mid-1982 BLADEX suffered a loss of over $300 million of commercial funding while central bank deposits, albeit very short term, increased by $120 million, thereby partially off-setting the decline in commercial bank funding.

The objectives of the two groups were clear. The central banks wanted to keep BLADEX in business while the international commercial banks, including the Class «C» shareholder banks, wanted to reduce their Latin American debt exposure. As BLADEX was the only Latin American institution which was meeting its interest and principal payment obligations on time, its success as a prudent lender made it the natural «target» of banks seeking to reduce their overall Latin American exposure.

As to the reason for their lack of confidence in BLADEX, this is not found in its record of non-performing or delinquent accounts. The total was $16 million at December 31, 1984, of which $10 million was to an Argentine State Agency which continues to pay interest. There may have been, however, a fear that with a shortening of the maturities of its liabilities, maturities were not matched with a medium-term portfolio of

$150 million and a declining balance of medium-term funding of $109 million plus capital. This was not unreasonable.

Despite all of this, in 1984 BLADEX continued to service its export customers. Total export financing outstanding at year-end was $360 million. More importantly, total disbursements during the year reached $1.0 billion, up from $0.8 billion in 1983 although down from the peak of $1.3 billion in 1982.

IFC, as the principal shareholder of BLADEX, was naturally concerned during this period. Earlier, BLADEX had been able to obtain both short and medium term financing, including three FRN issues in the Euromarket, without the need for IFC support.

It became clear during 1984, however, that with an increasing cost of funds, a shortening of terms, and growing dependence on its central bank shareholders, that there was a risk that BLADEX would have to reduce its export funding at a time when what was needed was an expansion. From IFC's perspective, further exports were crucial to the eventual solution to the Latin American debt crisis. Furthermore, while traditional exports would remain fundamental to this, non-traditional exports were of double importance at the margin. First, they were less affected by the adverse terms of trade than the traditional staples. Second, much of Latin America's fledgling industrial development in the private sector depended on them.

IFC, thus, had to find a way to help restore confidence in BLADEX, including both winning back the support of its traditional international bank lenders and finding new sources of funds.

Initial efforts in mid-1984 to syndicate a new medium term loan with the banks were unsuccessful despite IFC's willingness to commit $25 million of its own funds if the Class «C» banks and others would match that amount between them.

Coincidentally, during this period, IFC had also been discussing with various European and U.S. capital market institutions – pension funds, insurance companies, investments trusts, etc. – as well as investment banks the possibility of establishing an international trust whereby these institutions would invest in the trust and the trust would buy equity and securities in a wide range of developing countries. It became apparent from these discussions, and also from the successful launching of the IFC sponsored $60 million Korean Fund, Inc. in mid-1984, that the major capital market institutions were beginning to become actively interested in Third World countries on a selective basis.

Encouraged by this, IFC started sounding out some of these institutions on the possibility of a BLADEX financing. IFC obtained a mandate from BLADEX's Board of Directors in January 1985 to attempt such a financing and reiterated its commitment to participate to the extent of $25 million – in this instance as an underwriter.

By early March, IFC had prepared a draft prospectus and engaged in initial discussions with all of BLADEX's major bank shareholders with merchant bank affiliates as well as with a number of U.S., European and Japanese investment banks otherwise unassociated with BLADEX. It became apparent within a few weeks that very few of the shareholder banks would participate as a co-lead manager although a few in Europe and Latin America indicated a possible interest as underwriters.

Encouragement was initially received from shareholder investment banks as well as from three non-shareholder investment banks (US, Swiss and Japanese). There seemed a good possibility that the transaction could be completed with a size somewhat in excess of the $50 million proposed and with an all-in cost to BLADEX of possibly less than the 1½% over six months LIBOR agreed to. However, the withdrawal of one of the major underwriting participants was a major set back.

To bring the transaction back to life IFC assumed the role of lead manager with an underwriting commitment of $17 million and Goldman Sachs International Corp. became co-lead manager with a commitment of $15 million. Nomura International Limited, joined by Yamaichi International (Europe) Limited committed $5 million each. IFC also arranged commitments from the following institutions to complete a $50 million underwriting syndicate:

Algemene Bank Nederland N.V.
Banco de la Nación Argentina
Banco del Istmo, S.A. Panama
Banco do Brasil, S.A.
Bank Europäischer Genossenschaftsbanken (BEG)
California Commerce Bank
Handelsbank N.W. (Overseas) Ltd.
Nederlandsche Middenstandsbank N.V.

The success of the transaction was notable on three counts. Firstly, IFC was able to attract a number of major investment banks and commercial banks as underwriters who had no previous involvement with or commitment to BLADEX. Second, from amongst the shareholders', in addition to the two Dutch Banks a number of Latin American Banks participated thus making an important sign of confidence. Finally, a number of major large institutions from Europe and Japan participated as investors to the extent of in excess of $25 million. Further, Banco Roberts, an Argentine Class «C» shareholder, purchased $2 million on behalf of private investors – another important demonstration of confidence. The transaction was signed on April 15, 1985.

The first six months of 1985 thus have been marked by: first, an important financial break-through in terms of finding significant new medium term funding sources for BLADEX permitting it to close its maturity gap; second, the establishment of new management; and, third, the beginning again of the expansion of its export financing role which started in the last half of 1984.

For the future, much is in store. Firstly, the beginning of an effort to arrange special syndicated financial packages for individual shareholder banks, where other lenders would join BLADEX in the funding, with BLADEX acting as administrator of the funds. Secondly, there is likely to be another approach to the international capital markets for additional medium term funds, possibly involving some form of equity.

Finally, with a stronger equity base, and more medium term funds, BLADEX would be able to expand its pre and post export financing role – a major «gap» in the non-traditional export funding system.

Aussenwirtschaft, 41. Jahrgang (1986), Heft I, Grüsch: Rüegger, S.81–87

Co-operation with IFC: Experience of a European Investor

Dr. Max D. Amstutz
Managing Director and Vice Chairman of
the Executive Committee, «Holderbank» Financière

1. Debt Crisis and the Role of IFC

My company, «Holderbank» Financière, is active in the field of cement and related products on a worldwide scale, and has made in the past twenty years numerous and substantial investments in the third world. Our industry is highly capital intensive, and the difficulty often present in financing such massive investments has brought us in close contact with IFC, which has been and still is a partner in several of our ventures in developing countries. Our investments in these countries have of course been deeply affected by the worldwide recession and the following debt crisis over the past four years. Furthermore, on a personal level, I have been a founding member of the Swiss ad hoc Committee on International Debt Problems. The three facts – Holderbank's strong investment position in the developing world, our relationship with IFC and my personal involvement in the problems of international debt – lead me to make some fundamental remarks on the debt crisis and the role which in my opinion can be played by IFC in this context.

We all know by now that the debt problem in the third world has not been solved yet. By emergency measures, such as rescheduling of a country's debt by the international banking community, special credits by the multilateral financial institutions and forced reduction of imports by the affected countries, the worst has been avoided and the crash of our free world credit system has not taken place. We are all conscious, however, that a lasting solution of the problem requires much more than emergency measures, shock treatment and the patchwork process of dealing with difficult situations as they come up. What we need now is the re-establishment of growth in the third world. Without economic growth, there is no solution to the debt problem, and only a better use of the existing capacities in plants and human resources and the establishment of new ventures will produce the cash flows necessary to overcome the almost permanent crisis. Such economic growth depends on the availability of loan and equity capital. Everybody knows that the savings and thus the capital formation in the developing countries is not sufficient to guarantee this growth. Outside financing is indispensable. Therefore, the flow of financial resources from the industrial to the developing countries which in the past years and probably also in this year was negative, must be reversed. This implies the following measures:

- *The developing countries should continue to take the necessary steps to bring public finances and inflation under control,* to reduce the state sector in the economy and to lower the barriers hampering foreign private investment.
- *The trend towards trade protectionism in industrial countries must be stopped and reversed,* to allow for more international trade and more exports for the developing world.
- *Foreign private investment in the developing countries must be increased,* in order not only to bring in more resources into these countries, but to create the necessary equity basis for voluntary lending.
- *Forced lending must again be replaced by voluntary lending.* The rules of the authorities controlling bank activity in industrial countries regarding risk-taking should be relaxed, and the commercial banking system should find mechanisms which allow again to increase the lending levels to developing countries.

For the latter two steps – more foreign private investment and voluntary lending to be resumed – the re-establishment of confidence is necessary. This confidence, however, will only emerge if the lending and investment flow to these countries resumes, as a visible sign of regained creditworthiness. Thus, we are confronted with a *vicious circle* which must be broken.

I strongly believe that IFC is one of the most important and most appropriate instruments to achieve this goal. Since they are a lender of last resort and since it is one of their principles not to require a guarantee, they are accustomed to take high risks. And they have proven over many years that they can live successfully with such risks. As a matter of fact they are today one of the last resources of private financing left, in the absence of sufficient commercial credit facilities.

As a European private investor and based on our positive experience with IFC, I recommend that ways and means are explored *to expand the role and the resources of IFC.* The vicious circle of hampering risks and insufficient lending must be broken; IFC can contribute as no other institution to this difficult task.

2. Holderbank's Experience with IFC: Basic Aspects

Let me now come to the question of our experience with IFC as a financial partner in an industrial investment. Holderbank had or still has IFC as an equity partner and/or a lender in cement ventures – expansions or new plants – in the following countries (in the order of magnitude of the project): Brazil, Ecuador, Mexico, Colombia and Cyprus. The *attractivity* of IFC for a foreign investor can be summarized as follows:

- The project must be feasible and is investigated in full details, but *IFC accepts a degree of risk* as to the country and to the venture itself which might not always be acceptable to commercial banks.
- No *guaranties except mortgages are usually necessary,* and government guaranties are in all cases excluded; instead of a parent company guaranty which often is required for commercial bank lending, IFC requests a Project Funds Agreement, with which instrument we will deal later.
- We also believe that IFC offers a *political umbrella* not only to the foreign investor but also to the commercial banks participating as indirect lenders in a loan sindicated by IFC. In this context, IFC also seeks to ensure that foreign exchange is available to service the loan and repatriation requirements.
- IFC is *exempt from tax at source* on interest payments, a feature which makes an IFC-loan in many cases less expensive than a commercial loan.
- IFC also *participates up to 25% in the equity* of a project until a local investor can be found for it. As a shareholder, IFC does never exercise its voting right and not interfere with management, although they insist on receiving a wide range of pertinent information on progress of the project and, later, on business progress. Since it is often difficult to find local partners in the beginning of a project, this facility of IFC is a viable and satisfactory solution for the foreign investor.

There are also some *drawbacks* connected with an IFC partnership:

- *IFC insists that local LDC partners be included in the shareholding,* immediately or at a later stage. This does not affect a multinational company like ours which has as one of its principles to invite interested local people to participate in our ventures. But it might be considered a drawback for those foreign investors who, fearing to loose patent or know-how substance or for other reasons, insist on controlling 100% of the equity. In addition, the documentation that governs the stock sales to locals, necessary if an immediate local participation is not possible, can be very difficult to draft and thus represent a time-consuming and complex task involving hard negotiation between the sponsor and IFC.
- In the absence of a parent company guaranty, *IFC usually requires in addition to the normal Investment Agreement, a Project Funds Agreement* which, to put it simply, commits the sponsor to invest additional funds in case the project incurs an overrun. This document is often difficult to negotiate because there may exist very different views regarding the risks of the project, and the sponsor might not be ready to commit, even hypothetically, more funds to the project than he thinks are necessary. The Project Funds Agreement, in this sense, represents a drawback. On the other hand, however, it offers a not to be neglected reward to the investor for going through this exercise by security off-balance sheet financing which probably, in the case of an overrun, would not be available elsewhere.

3. Holderbank's Experience with IFC: Operational Aspects

Throughout the past 15 years, Holderbank and certain subsidiaries and associated companies had a close and extensive relationship with IFC in the field of establishing feasibility studies for new or expansion projects, of negotiating financing terms, of setting up financial agreements and carrying through these agreements, often in a changing economic environment and with unforeseen situations coming up. In the following, I will try to summarize and evaluate the experience which Holderbank made in this *operational relationship* with IFC.

The bureaucratic aspects

It is often assumed that dealing with a multilateral, politically based financial institution such as IFC, is a *complicated, lengthy and frustrating process* full of obstacles. While we believe that certain parts of the negotiation and decision process are indeed lengthy and wearisome, this is by far *not true* for the whole process as such.

Our experience shows that *IFC disposes of a staff which is specially competent and diligent* in the field of analysing the feasibility of projects and advising the investor in the matter of putting together a suitable financial package to fund these projects. I would even say that due to the specialized knowledge and the vast experience of IFC in financing private investments in developing countries, their competence in this particular field exceeds that of many banks. Thus, it is *generally an easy and relatively fast process* to put the project features and the financing together and to negotiate the financial terms (always provided that the project is economically feasible).

What we might consider somewhat lengthy and cumbersome is the *legal work involved and the decision process in the IFC.* There seem to be more approval levels than an investor would confront at a commercial bank. Approvals are essentially based on a review by the *Investment Committee,* and the investor *never knows for sure whether he has a deal* until the Committee approves the project. I would like to point out, however, that due to the debt situation in third world countries, the decision process in commercial banks makes it much more difficult today to get fast approval of loans for ventures in developing countries, unless a solid parent company guaranty is made available. This means that *the gap in fast approval* that might have existed in the past between IFC and commercial banks is *narrowing.*

A last bureaucratic aspect: During the lifetime of an IFC loan, quite a *substantial documentation* on project progress and, later, on business progress is required periodically and frequently. This paperwork is cumbersome. However, here again we may say that after initial difficulties a routine is usually established and the information generated serves also the company issuing it.

The aspects of flexibility

We live today in a political, social, economic and monetary environment which is *exposed to unforeseen and rapid changes* throughout the world. In order to cope successfully with these changes, we have to *adapt our financial policies and sometimes also the financial structure* of our companies to the new circumstances. A high degree of flexibility is required. What is our experience with IFC in this respect?

The debt crisis in Latin America has given us some valuable indications in this field. For example, IFC has shown *understanding and helpfulness* in a case where insufficient market growth has hampered the financial potential of one of our companies and has reacted well to the request for changing the terms and conditions set up in the original contract. We have been confirmed in our belief that IFC, in spite of being a political creation, *operates with a private sector orientation.* And since their charter commits them to venture and to create, they are able to take *somewhat more risks than commercial banks.* These are in our opinion the two reasons for the fact that they are generally flexible when confronted with change. The decision process, however, is also in these cases rather time-consuming, for the same reasons we mentioned earlier.

However, some of the general policy terms which IFC invariably applies to all the financial arrangements could be considered as being too rigid. Thus, a *Commitment fee* of one percent is mandatory on undisbursed portions of a loan, and the interest rate is always a *fixed rate,* the company taking the loan having no option to choose a fixed or a variable rate. These conditions should, in may opinion, be overhauled in view of the rapidly changing conditions of financial markets and the debt problems affecting developing countries.

Conclusion

Today's economic environment in the developing countries is suffering from a still prevailing absence of confidence, high risks and hence a lack of sufficient investment and growth. To return to confidence and growth, which represent the greatest needs for economic and social progress in the third world, sound and stable monetary policies must be established in the LDC's, trade protectionism in industrial countries eliminated, a positive and sufficient flow of funds towards the third world both in the form of equity and loan money restored and the private sector development revitalized. In this context, IFC has an important role to play, because it unites three characteristics which are difficult to find for an investor in today's environment: it is ready to assume risk without burdening the investor with prohibitive charges and guaranties, it finances not only debt but also equity, both very scarce resources at this time, and it is a stable partner also in difficult situations. This statement is fully supported by our experience.

Aussenwirtschaft, 41. Jahrgang (1986), Heft I, Grüsch: Rüegger, S.89–96

Funding Direct Investment through Cofinancing: The Commercial Banker's View

Dr. Klaus Huber
Senior Vice President, Union Bank of Switzerland

Introduction and Outline

There can be little doubt that forging the policies and programs which will allow developing countries (LDC's) to move on to the next phase in managing their debt problem is of utmost urgency. I am referring to the stage of transition from austerity to revival of development and growth as many countries reach their socio-political limits of further demand management and import squeeze policies à la IMF.

The proposal of U.S. Treasury Secretary Baker – a $29 billion increase in capital flows by commercial banks and multilateral development banks (MDB's) to the 15 most indebted LDC's – seconded by declarations from many north and south officials as well as multinational agency heads at the IMF-meeting stressed the importance of concerted resumption of lending by *both* the public and private sectors and the need to revive the private sector in and foreign private direct investment to LDC's.

Few people seem to question the basic wisdom of these policies which, for lack of any better name, I would like to call «The Spirit of Seoul». However, when it comes to committing substantial new funds both commercial banks and private investors ask the legitimate question: Why should we? What are the credit enhancements or added security to justify such a commitment to bank shareholders, depositors or regulators who collectively pressure the commercial banks to improve their capital-asset ratios and improve the quality of their assets?

The fact is that banks and investors alike are still suffering from a bad case of indigestion regarding their exposure to developing countries. In my view progress has to be made in the following 3 areas, before «The Spirit of Seoul» will convince private capital to start flowing voluntarily back to the LDC's:

■ First, remove the constraints that LDC's have towards foreign direct investment such as outright prohibition of foreign control, restrictions on dividend and interest remittances, and erratic financial and exchange rate policies;
■ Second, foster the promotion of domestic private investment by selling to the private sector industries previously held in the public hand; a number of ongoing efforts in countries such as Turkey, Malaysia and Singapore are already showing positive results! However, we do not have to look that far for inspiration: Mrs. Thatcher's policies for privatizing British industry are well on their way!
■ Third, introduce innovative approaches to risk sharing between the private and public sectors such as cofinancing with MDB's, private and public insurance schemes (including the recently created Multilateral Investment Guarantee Agency).

1. Historic Capital Flows and Future Needs for Resumption of Development

Historic flows are characterized by two major shifts:

- First, from equity to debt; and
- second, from public to private capital.

The relative share of private equity investment, while increasing in absolute terms throughout the 1970's, dropped from 20% to 9% in 1970/83. Since 1981 it was falling from $17 billion to $8 billion in 1983. Ready availability of bank loans resulting from the recycling of OPEC money and low or negative real interest rates were the main underlying factors in favor of increased private capital flows. It was accompanied by a large increase in export credits, which maintained its share in total flows.

Future capital requirements (1985-90) are examined in the World Bank's recently published «Development Report 1985» which gives an estimate of LDC's new financing requirements for a successful transition from recovery to sustained non-inflationary growth. The recipe for success implies restoring monetary and fiscal balance in *industrial countries* to reduce interest rates while opening their import markets to *LDC's;* this would allow the latter to reduce their debt service burden while continuing with structural adjustment efforts of economic pricing, exchange and trade policies.

Without a resumption of capital flows from whatever sources, the LDC's will simply not have the means to finance reforms and invest in productive capacity. The high scenario projected capital flows illustrates how the various sources of capital could contribute. Clearly, private investment should again become more prominent than in the recent past; but private banks, MDB's, Official Development Assistance (ODA) and export credits will also have to carry their weight.

I am absolutely convinced that, under present circumstances, LDC's would be well served if they were to open their door again more aggressively to let foreign equity investment in: Real interest rates are at historic highs thus pushing up significantly the cost of borrowing. Equity capital could take a larger share of the exchange and interest risk of foreign capital while, at the same time, providing important technology and management benefits.

On the other hand, there are limitations to the role of foreign equity investment. It can only be a complement and not a replacement to borrowed money. It is linked to specific investment projects and cannot be used flexibly to finance the broad needs of development. Take today's low capacity utilization in most LDC's following an adjustment program: To revive the economy you do not need new investment in many cases but working capital injections to buy spare parts or improved intermediary goods! Also, equity investment tends to concentrate on a few sectors in the resource and manufacturing industries and, moreover, on the larger economies providing substantial internal markets.

2. Experience with Cofinancing: A Swiss View

Cofinancing with MDB's has become an important method of channeling funds to high priority projects in developing countries and it is receiving increasing attention from commercial banks. Traditionally, Swiss banks (and for that matter many European banks) have directed their lending to LDC's mainly in support of their internationally active domestic clients. Thus, their LDC-portfolio mainly consists of export credits, a substantial part of which is covered by official export credit insurance. To a lesser degree it includes assets with the subsidiaries of Swiss companies in these countries. But only occasionally have the Swiss banks participated in the sovereign lending which was so much en vogue in the 70's and early 80's. This is not to say that the Swiss Banks would not have their share in rescheduled LDC debt. But in proportion to their capital and reserves, total assets or any other yardstick, it is quite a manageable order of magnitude.

Cofinancing with MDB's is a more recent phenomenon in the Swiss banking community. Union Bank of Switzerland (UBS), for instance, which had participated in only a handful of cofinancings with IFC and the World Bank in the late 70's, took the policy decision in 1980, to set up a professional lending unit for project and cofinancing. In the meantime we have become quite busy. Roughly one third of our project finance portfolio, which is roughly half the size of our export credit portfolio, is with borrowers in LDC's. Of that, about a dozen loans are cofinancings and virtually all of them with the IFC.

Based on our experience with cofinancing I would like to draw some generally valid conclusions. Let me preface these comments by giving you first five policy reasons, why UBS participates in cofinancing with MDB's. They are, not necessarily by order of importance:

- First, projects are appraised (and often prepared) by the MDB and meet their high technical, financial and economic standards;
- second, the presence of the MDB offers a political *«umbrella»* or *«comfort blanket»* whereby the risk of negative government interference in the project (expropriation, fiscal or tariff action, etc.,) is greatly diminished;
- third, MDB's can act as an *«honest broker»* bringing together the often diverging views and interests of foreign investors, co-lenders and host government and/or private sector parties thus greatly enhancing the project's success rate;
- fourth, MDB's (and in particular IFC) often obtain a *«priority in payment» status* in LDC's, whereby the central bank makes foreign exchange (forex) available for the MDB's before other lenders; in case of the World Bank cofinancing scheme, the same effect is reached through *«cross default clauses»* whereby the World Bank can call its loan in default in case of a payment default with the commercial bank;
- fifth, if the project gets into difficulties, the MDB as a concerned investor and lender is available to restructure the project with technical advice (including technical performance appraisals, revisions of business plans, legal advice, etc.) and possibly injection of new funds (equity, quasi-equity or loans).

How does all this work out in practice? What was the track record of our cofinanced loans, particularly in countries which have since rescheduled? Let me summarize some of our experiences, which are admittedly still limited, as some of the loans are still disbursing:

■ The IFC «umbrella» providing preferential debt service treatment even in rescheduling situations has worked without fault! If the borrower was able to generate local currency, we always got paid in foreign exchange, albeit not always exactly on time. Thus from past experience one can conclude that IFC's umbrella provides effective protection against *transfer risk*. Unfortunately, the same cannot be said for the «old-style» World Bank cofinancings with commercial banks. Several were cought in some of the recent reschedulings. This is deplorable, as it at least psychologically also weakens the image of the «new style» – and admittedly much more strongly structured – World Bank cofinancing instruments.

■ *Technically,* all of our cofinanced projects are on schedule and within budget; some have been completed, others are still under construction, but the high quality of IFC's technical work pays out. Which, incidentally is no substitute for doing our own technical, financial and commercial analysis by UBS' engineers and bankers. But it certainly cuts down the workload!

■ However, not all of the projects have escaped the *commercial* risk resulting from local recession, price controls and austerity measures: at 50% capacity utilization and prices heading deep south, as was the case with two of our cement plants in Latin America, it is virtually impossible to generate enough cash flow to keep debt service coverage ratios above unity. So, we are learning the hard way about some of the gray areas between political risk (including the effects of government macro policies) and commercial risk. So far, the rescheduling needs have been minimal, certainly far below what has become customary with general country reschedulings.

■ Finally, if there is one area where we would like to strengthen our ties with the MDB's it is in *project supervision and control;* as a participant in an IFC loan, the commercial bank has normally no direct access to the borrower for project follow-up. This task is left to IFC which, as an equity holder, understandably may not always have exactly the same objectives as the pure lender. Since risk minimization or risk avoidance in project lending, where lenders normally have only recourse to project assets but not to the sponsor's guarantee, is tantamount to the ability to react quickly, commercial lenders naturally feel constrained if they cannot act directly.

All told, I believe our past experience with cofinancing has been beneficial to both lenders, borrowers as well as sponsors/equity holders for whose «benefit» or relationship we enter the cofinancing operation in the first place. However, as LDC lending risk increases while the call for new money (Baker Proposal) is addressed loud and clear to the commercial and multilateral development banking community, I believe new techniques or initiatives for risk distribution and sharing are called for.

3. Agenda for New or Enhanced Risk Sharing Techniques in Project Finance

Before entering into some concrete proposals, let me briefly review the risk sharing patterns among risk carriers in a project. As one would expect, each project or investment has unique risk characteristics and, therefore, also a unique risk sharing solution. Nevertheless by oversimplification, it has been past practice for banks to take at least part of the *political* risks while offloading the other, often larger part with the official (more recently also the private) insurance market. In export financing, typically the exporter always carries part of the political risk not covered by the official risk insurance scheme.

Commercial risks, on the other hand, would typically be shared between banks, sponsors/borrowers and product buyers. *Before completion,* the risks are normally with sponsors. *After completion,* the banks are normally willing to absorb technology and market risks, often supported by off-take agreements from product buyers. The latter is a must in most mining, pipeline and utility projects.

In view of the recent deterioration of creditworthiness of many LDC's in the wake of the debt crisis, the above risk sharing formulas are no longer sufficient to mobilize new voluntary capital in the magnitudes spelled out by Secretary Baker. Let's therefore have a look at four possible *ways to enhance credit and/or investment risk* through new or revamped old approaches:

■ First, *Off-Shore Escrows:* This is an old instrument which, however, is being revived in the context of foreign exchange earning projects. Forex receipts are kept off-shore, outside the control of the central bank of the host country to assure that debt service (and often other forex requirements of the project) can be met, thus effectively eliminating the transfer risk. Combined with a borrowing vehicle kept off-shore, one can also effectively eliminate the rescheduling risk.

■ Second, *MDB Forex Guarantees:* import substitution projects do not lend themselves to the above security mechanism. However, they can be equally critical to improve an LDC's forex situation. Take the example of an onshore gas field, the output of which will be used for domestic electricity generation. The gas field, developed by a foreign oil company, can be financed by commercial bank funds only if a guarantee mechanism can be put in place to secure the performance of the long-term off-take agreement with the government owned utility, the project's principal credit support. Cofinancing with a MDB, whereby the latter backs up a commercial credit line covering say one or two years of debt service, could provide the solution of an otherwise unbankable project. This novel approach is presently being considered by the World Bank which could yield similar solutions in many other projects (e.g. oil export projects which initially produce for domestic use only).

■ Third, *Multilateral Investment Guarantee Agency (MIGA):* The new investment guarantee scheme of the World Bank Group approved at the Seoul-Meeting together with government or private insurance schemes such as OPIC in the US, AIG in the US or Lloyds in London, will also have to be used more frequently to provide credit support with its political risk coverage. If ratified by the member governments, MIGA will greatly increase the possibilities in a market which has become much more difficult – and expensive! – in recent years. This would be particularly true if MIGA were to provide long-term cover in line with project cash flow requirements, something which the private market with its present limit of three years cannot meet.

■ Fourth, *Enhanced Cofinancing Credit Support:* The existing cofinancing schemes of the World Bank and IFC, on a case by case basis, could also be made stronger to attract more voluntary commercial bank funding. In particular, I am thinking of using the World Bank's guarantee authority more frequently, for instance by increasing its share in the B-Loan by taking a larger portion of the longer maturities. To some extent this new technique has been used in two recent IBRD loans in Chile and Uruguay in connection with a rescheduling package, thereby successfully attracting «voluntary» commercial bank funding. IFC, on the other hand, could make the security structures of some of its B-Loans stronger, by requiring sponsor support beyond project completion (thus effectively making it a corporate loan) or by injecting a higher proportion of risk capital (equity or quasi-equity).

Some of the above suggestions I have made have to be refined and strengthened to be able to weather the heavy storms of LDC credit risks. But I am convinced that this is the direction all participants in the international lending and investment community, MDB's, governments, insurance companies, sponsors and commercial bankers – have to move, if the *Spirit of Seoul* is to become a reality bringing the LDC's back to the path of sustained growth and development.

Part III

Protection of Foreign Private Investment

Aussenwirtschaft, 41. Jahrgang (1986), Heft I, Grüsch: Rüegger, S.99–104

Investment Protection Treaties: Recent Trends and Prospects

Dr. Hans-Martin Burkhardt
Ministerial Secretary, Ministry of Economics, Bonn

Investment protection treaties are attracting increasing interest from developing nations and industrialized countries alike. Today, far more than 200 agreements of this sort are in existence worldwide. While adequate investment protection is not as important in arriving at the decision to invest abroad as are factors such as growth potential, market size, and host country infrastructure, it is, however, a major determinant of a country's investment climate.

The growing interest which the developing nations are visibly taking in investment protection treaties is consequently related to their increasing willingness to host foreign investment. The debt crisis in the Third World is undoubtedly playing an additional role. The interest in direct investment is rising as the flow of bank lending is drying up.

To no small extent, the industrialized countries view the model of a worldwide network of bilateral investment protection treaties as a certain alternative to the application of the rules of customary international law in the field of investment protection, as these rules are questioned by the developing nations. There need be no contradiction in the behavior of Third World countries which one day practice group solidarity by voting in favor of a United Nations resolution criticizing foreign investment and the day after conclude an investment protection treaty. These treaties are regarded as an element of bilateral economic cooperation.

1. Historical Development

Investment protection was long granted within the framework of the Friendship, Commerce, and Navigation treaties which the United States in particular concluded with both industrial and developing nations. After the second World War, when trading issues were largely settled multilaterally within the framework of GATT, there arose an increasing need to conclude specific investment protection agreements. In some countries, such as Switzerland and the Netherlands, investment protection rules were also incorporated to some extent into agreements on economic cooperation.

Three post-War phases may be distinguished. The first investment protection treaties were concluded by the Federal Republic of Germany in 1959 and by Switzerland in 1961. It is, perhaps, no coincidence that neither of the two was a colonial power, that neither was able to protect its foreign investments by close historical ties.

Later, during the Seventies, the example of these two countries was followed by a number of other European nations. Above all, France, the United Kingdom, Belgium/Luxembourg, and the Netherlands concluded investment protection treaties.

Then, toward the end of the Seventies, Japan and the United States, the two major non-European economic powers, began to take an interest in investment protection treaties. Japan, despite its high level of investment abroad, has nevertheless concluded only two such agreements to date — with Egypt in 1977 and Sri Lanka in 1982. In the latter year, the United States began a series of intensive negotiations on investment protection accords and has signed more than a dozen treaties to date.

It is interesting to note that a number of treaties have in the meantime been concluded by developing countries. The Asian-African Legal Consultative Committee has drafted model treaties for such agreements between developing countries, largely patterned on the model treaties between industrialized and developing states.

Multilateral attempts to establish fixed rules for investment protection have thus far offered little promise of success. Current efforts within the framework of the United Nations Code of Conduct for Transnational Corporations to include rules for host countries' treatment of foreign investment are to be assessed with considerable scepticism.

Regional approaches would seem to present the greater prospects of success. In 1984, the Organization of the Islamic Conference adopted a Convention for the Protection and Promotion of Investment between Islamic Countries. Within the context of the Euro-Arab Dialogue, negotiations between the Member States of the European Community and the Arab League on a convention for investment protection are far advanced. What is special about this convention is that it not only addresses itself to direct investment but includes all types of financial investment within its clauses on protection. In the Lomé III Convention between the Member States of the European Community and 66 developing nations, for the most part African countries, the importance of bilateral investment protection treaties has been expressly reasserted. In this case, the principle of non-discrimination is recognized; that is, countries already having concluded an investment protection treaty may not discriminate against investors from other signatory countries.

2. Provisions of Investment Protection Treaties

At the heart of the investment protection treaties are the guarantees for compensation in the case of expropriation, free transfer of capital and earnings, national treatment, most favored nation treatment, and international arbitration.

The United States new model treaty differs from the classic European treaties in one important point. The goal of the American treaties is not only the protection of licensed investment but also the highest possible degree of freedom for capital transactions. The foreign investor is to have entry to the host country on a par with domestic investors. Performance requirements are not to be imposed on his activity and he is not to be placed at competitive disadvantage to state-run enterprises in the host country. The right of free establishment as provided for in the old Friendship, Commerce, and Navigation treaties has been adopted here.

The Free Transfer of Capital and Earnings

The transfer guarantee repeatedly turns up as the object of lengthy and difficult negotiations. The guarantee covers convertibility, i.e. availability of freely convertible currency for the intended transfer. Owing to the shortage of hard currency faced by many developing nations, there have been various approaches taken toward solving this problem.

The easiest, albeit poorest, solution is to regulate the transfer by national legislation governing currency transactions. A «guarantee» of this nature is of no interest to the investor and contradicts the purpose of a treaty under international law, which is to provide guarantees independent of national legislation.

A reference to the rights and duties of members of the Agreement on the International Monetary Fund is also not sufficient to achieve the purpose of an investment protection treaty. The IMF agreement contains no rules for free capital movement and it is possible to receive IMF approval for restrictions on current transactions. Above all, it should be taken into account that most of the developing nations, upon accession to the IMF agreement, made use of the possibility to retain existing national restrictions on capital transfers. In these cases, reference to the rights deriving from the IMF agreement amounts to making capital transfers subject to national statutes on foreign currency transactions.

In a number of bilateral treaties, the following compromise solution has been concluded: in cases in which a country encounters extraordinary balance of payments difficulties, certain restrictions on transfers may be made. But this does not apply to the transfers of earnings, and to this extent, the solution follows the approach also contained in the IMF agreement, which provides for a stricter system for current payments. By contrast, the retransfer of capital can be «stretched» over several years. An annual minimum transfer (usually 20%) must, however, be guaranteed. This solution, found in some German and, more recently, also in some British treaties, has been incorporated into the draft of a Euro-Arab Investment Protection Convention and in the model treaty drafted by the Asian-African Legal Consultative Committee.

More than ever before, the transfer guarantee has now become an important investment incentive. In allocating scarce resources, developing nations with serious interests in hosting foreign investment will assign priority to the transfer of funds relating to such investment and provide corresponding transfer guarantees. In practice, however, the foreign investor will more likely need hard currency to import pre-materials and spare parts than to transfer profits. It is therefore of interest to note that the Netherlands has recently included the transfer of hard currency for this purpose within its investment protection treaties.

National Treatment

National treatment is also a regular bone of contention between the industrialized countries and the developing nations. It should first be pointed out that the Latin American concept of national treatment, which at best provides for equal treatment of foreign investors and by no means allows them to receive better treatment than nationals, is not the subject of discussion here. Distinct from the Latin American approach is the classic concept of national treatment, according to which foreigners are treated no less favorably than nationals. The scheme for treatment of nationals is regarded as a minimum. International law is binding whenever it provides for a higher protective standard for the foreigner. The Latin American understanding of national treatment entails the negation of customary international law in connection with the treatment of foreign investors.

The developing countries' main objection to national treatment is based on the idea that, in developing domestic industry, domestic enterprises should receive particular consideration, more so than the large multinational enterprises from the industrial countries. Accordingly, in the framework of the Asian-African Legal Consultative Committee, the idea as to whether national treatment should be restricted to investment between developing nations has been debated. Experience shows that the industrial countries have repeatedly been willing to make exceptions from the general principle of national treatment and allow specific support measures for domestic companies in developing nations. But the principle of the prohibition of arbitrary discrimination must be retained. This prohibition is gaining in practical importance as host countries supervise and regulate the activity of foreign investors. Incidentally, making a distinction between nationals and foreigners would be contrary to the joint venture concept particularly propagated by the developing countries.

3. Investment Guarantees instead of Investment Protection?

In connection with the adoption of the Convention on a Multilateral Investment Guarantee Agency (MIGA), this question has assumed acute importance. Countries which believe that all indigenous efforts toward improving the investment climate are superfluous since the investor can insure himself against risks, are victim to a misunderstanding of great consequence. A solid investment climate is not created by insuring against certain risks but by removing investment barriers and providing the investor with reliable guarantees. The security provided by investment protection treaties, by the way, applies to all investments, whether or not they are insured and it extends beyond the risks covered by investment insurance. The only legitimate question is the connection that should be made between investment protection and a guarantee system. This has thus far been a matter of dispute, also within the negotiations for the MIGA.

Some countries, such as the Federal Republic of Germany and France, make it a matter of principle to conclude investment protections treaties or at least comparable investment protection as the prerequisite for taking on a guarantee. Countries which have negotiated only relatively few treaties naturally do not impose such requirements. In the past, the United States (and Canada as well) have considered the agreements between OPIC, the American insurance company, and the host countries to be sufficient. The OPIC agreements basically contain arrangements for arbitration; they do not provide for material investment protection rules.

In the MIGA Convention, the principle of legal protection by the host country was finally adopted upon the insistance of some industrial countries. The protective standard required for assumption of the guarantee is, however, still an open question. We can only hope that MIGA is not striving for the competitive edge over the national guarantee systems by waiving demands for comparable legal protection.

Aussenwirtschaft, 41. Jahrgang (1986), Heft I, Grüsch: Rüegger, S.105–122

The Role of ICSID and the Projected Multilateral Investment Guarantee Agency (MIGA)

Dr. Ibrahim F. I. Shihata
Vice-President and General Counsel, The World Bank
Secretary-General, International Centre for Settlement of Investment Disputes

I. Introduction

The aim of this article is to examine two important initiatives the World Bank has taken to accomplish its objective of stimulating increased foreign private investment. With a period of 20 years separating their respective approvals, these initiatives took the form of establishing two international organizations, the International Centre for Settlement of Investment Disputes (ICSID), whose constituent instrument was approved in 1965, and the Multilateral Investment Guarantee Agency (MIGA) approved in October 1985 by the World Bank's Board of Governors.

ICSID provides facilities for conciliation and arbitration of investment disputes. MIGA will issue guarantees for investments against non-commercial risks and provide a wide range of promotional activities. However, ICSID should not be regarded merely as a forum for resolving disputes and MIGA should not be seen simply as an insurance scheme. The broad objective of both ICSID and MIGA is to promote increased international investment through the improvement of investment conditions in the host countries. The protection ICSID and MIGA offer to foreign private investment is best understood in the context of this broad objective.

II. The Role of the International Centre for Settlement of Investment Disputes

A. Background

It is clear that the fear of political risks often inhibits investment flows to developing countries, despite the availability of attractive investment opportunities in such countries. Beginning in the late 1950s, a number of international schemes were proposed to address this problem. One possibility was the establishment of an international agency which would provide insurance to investors against non-commercial risks. This concept was discussed in the early 1960s in various international fora, such as the World Bank and the Organisation for Economic Co-operation and Development. For a variety of reasons, however, the early inititatives to create such an insurance facility did not materialize. Meanwhile, the World Bank's management had, in 1961, suggested that a special forum for the settlement of disputes involving private parties could contribute to further encouraging the flow of private capital into developing countries.[1] Extensive preparatory work and consultations on this possibility followed. By 1964, the prospects for negotiating a convention establishing the dispute settlement facility appeared favorable. Accordingly, the Board of Governors of the World Bank directed the Bank's Executive Directors to formulate such a convention and submit it to governments together with such recommendations as the Executive Directors might deem appropriate.[2] Pursuant to this directive, the Executive Directors, assisted by a Committee of experts comprising representatives from sixty-one governments, formulated the Convention on the Settlement of Investment Disputes between States and Nationals of Other States (the ICSID Convention)[3] and submitted it to member governments of the World Bank in March of 1965 «for consideration with a view to signature and ratification, acceptance or approval». The ICSID Convention has since been signed by ninety-one countries of which eighty-seven are already Contracting States. An examination of some of the main features of the system created by the ICSID Convention will help to explain this positive development.

---

[1] See Address of World Bank President Eugene R. Black, 1961 Annual Meetings of the Boards of Governors of the International Bank for Reconstruction and Development and the International Development Association *Summary Proceedings* 7, 8-9 (1961).

[2] See 2 *Convention on the Settlement of Investment Disputes between States and Nationals of Other States – Documents concerning the Origin and Formulation of the Convention* 608 (1968).

[3] The ICSID Convention, 575 U.N.T.S. 159, along with the text of the Executive Directors' *Report* thereon, is reproduced in 4 *Int'l Legal Materials* 524 (1965).

B. ICSID's Voluntary Character

The facilities provided by the Centre established by the ICSID Convention are, in the first place, available on a voluntary basis. States eligible to join ICSID (members of the World Bank and States invited to sign the ICSID Convention under its Article 67) are obviously free to decline to do so. Their decision has no bearing on their relations with the World Bank itself. Moreover, ratification of the ICSID Convention is only an expression of a Contracting State's willingness, in principle, to make use of the ICSID machinery. Ratification does not constitute an obligation to use that machinery. That obligation can arise only after the Contracting State concerned has specifically agreed to submit to ICSID arbitration a particular dispute or class of disputes.

Under Article 25(4) of the Convention, any Contracting State may in addition notify ICSID, either at the time of ratification or at any time thereafter, of the class or classes of disputes that it would or would not consider arbitrable under ICSID's auspices.[1]

Within this framework, parties have considerably more freedom to determine whether their transaction is suitable for ICSID arbitration than might be assumed from the limitation of the Centre's jurisdiction to investment disputes of a legal character. The Convention does not define the term «investment», and this lack of definition, which was deliberate, has enabled the Convention to accommodate both traditional types of investment in the form of capital contributions and new types of investment including service contracts and transfers of technology. Disputes submitted to the Centre have ranged from disputes relating to the exploitation of natural resources to disputes arising out of management contracts or technical and licensing agreements.[2] Most of the disputes submitted to ICSID, it may be added, related to genuine contractual disputes concerning the interpretation of investment agreements or matters of performance. Only a few concerned unilateral termination of investment agreements, e.g., in the form of outright nationalization or the revocation of investment licenses. Interestingly, no disputes relating to financial transactions have been submitted to the Centre. Parties are, of course, also free to decide not to submit their investment disputes to ICSID, and although

---

[1] So far, only 5 States (Israel, Jamaica, Guyana, Papua New Guinea and Saudi Arabia) have made such notifications. The texts of their notifications may be found in *Measures taken by Contracting States for the Purpose of the Convention,* ICSID Doc. ICSID/8-C (March 1985).

[2] Summary information on the disputes so far submitted to ICSID is available in *ICSID Cases, 1972-1984,* ICSID Doc. ICSID/16 (February 1985).

provision for ICSID arbitration is sometimes made in transnational loans to foreign governments, it is no secret that lenders often continue to require the judicial adjudication of loan disputes before the domestic courts of New York or London.[1]

C. Flexibility of the ICSID System

Second, the ICSID system is highly flexible. Parties may derogate from the rules applicable to ICSID proceedings in order to accommodate their particular needs. For example, most of the provisions regarding the number of arbitrators and the method for their appointment are permissive, and apply only in the absence of agreement between the parties. While they have the necessary flexibility, the ICSID rules are specific enough to ensure that a party cannot frustrate the proceedings. For example, if one of the parties refuses to cooperate in the appointment of arbitrators, the tribunal may still be constituted through the appointment of arbitrators by the President of the World Bank in his capacity as Chairman of ICSID's Administrative Council. Even if a party fails to participate in the proceedings, the Convention ensures that the proceedings can continue[2] and lead to an award. In practice, there has been little occasion for these provisions to be used, in view of the high degree of State participation in the proceedings and of their frequent termination by means of amicable settlement.

D. Effectiveness of the ICSID System

Third, the ICSID system is uniquely effective. While parties are free to decide whether to make use of the ICSID machinery, the ICSID Convention (Article 25 [1]) assures both parties that once they have consented to submit disputes to ICSID conciliation or arbitration, neither party can unilaterally revoke its consent. The exclusivity of the ICSID system also contributes to its effectiveness. Under the ICSID Convention (Article 26), consent of the parties to ICSID arbitration is deemed to be exclusive of any other remedy, unless the parties otherwise agree. This rule has several consequences, one of which is that ICSID proceedings are insulated in all Contracting States from any form of judicial intervention or control.

---

1 See G. Delaume, «ICSID and the Banker», *Int'l Fin. L. Rev.* 9 (October 1983).
2 ICSID Convention, Art. 45(2).

The ICSID Convention furthermore assures the effectiveness of an ICSID award once it has been rendered. Article 53(1) of the Convention provides that such an award is binding on the parties, while Article 54(2) provides that a party may obtain recognition and enforcement of the award by furnishing a certified copy thereof to the competent court or other authority designated for the purpose by each Contracting State. This simple procedure eliminates the problems of the recognition and enforcement of foreign arbitral awards, which subsist in domestic laws and under other international conventions. Under the ICSID Convention, there is no exception to the binding character of ICSID awards and the role of the courts of Contracting States is purely to assist in the recognition of ICSID awards.

The ICSID Convention does not, however, derogate from the rules of immunity from execution that may prevail in a Contracting State.[1] It is thus possible that an ICSID award could be executed against the assets of the State (or of one of its subdivisions or agencies) party to the dispute in certain Contracting States and not in other Contracting States. This is an issue which has been the subject of much academic debate. But it has not arisen in practice and is unlikely to arise. Reliance by the State in question upon its immunity from execution would be contrary to its obligation under the Convention to comply with the award and would expose that State to various sanctions set forth in the Convention.[2] Moreover, refusal by the State involved to comply with an ICSID award would deprive it of credibility in the international business community. This is not a risk that a State would be likely to assume lightly.

It should be recalled that out of twenty-two ICSID proceedings, nine of which are currently pending, five only have resulted in an award on the merits and eight have been either discontinued or amicably settled. This high proportion of settlements is consistent with the objectives of ICSID. It should increase as a result of the availability of a new «prehearing» conference procedure offered under the revised ICSID Arbitration Rules.[3] By providing opportunities for candid reappraisals by the parties of the merits of their respective claims, such conferences should help in further promoting amicable settlements.

---

[1] *Id.*, Art. 55

[2] Including the resumption of diplomatic protection hitherto suspended under the ICSID Convention and the right of the Contracting State whose national is a party to the dispute to bring an international claim against the non-complying State.

[3] See Rule 21 of the Rules of Procedure for Arbitration Proceedings (Arbitration Rules) as revised on September 26, 1984, reproduced in *ICSID Basic Documents* 61, ICSID Doc. ICSID/15 (January 1985).

The effectiveness of ICSID cannot, at any rate, be assessed only on the basis of the number of disputes that have been submitted to or settled by that institution. When an ICSID clause provides for compulsory arbitration, it is to be assumed that the prospect of involvement in such proceedings will work as a deterrent to the actions which give rise to the institution of proceedings and as an incentive to amicable settlement through negotiations.

E. Balance of Interests of the ICSID System

Beyond providing a mechanism for the settlement of investment disputes that is voluntary, flexible and effective, the strength of the ICSID system lies in the careful balance it maintains between the interests and requirements of all the parties involved. The arrangements made for ICSID's governing body, the Administrative Council, reflect this balance of interests. The Council consists of one representative of each Contracting State. As each representative casts one vote, the ICSID Convention assures equal representation to all Contracting States.

The ICSID Convention is unique in giving private investors direct access to an international forum. Investors are assured that refusal or abstention by the State party to the dispute to participate in the proceedings after it has given its consent cannot frustrate the ICSID arbitral process. When the ICSID Convention was formulated, it was realized that a balance would have to be struck in respect of such advantages. The Executive Directors of the World Bank pointed out that:

> «When a host State consents to the submission of a dispute with investor to the Centre, thereby giving the investor direct access to an international jurisdiction, the investor should not be in a position to ask his state to espouse his case and that State should not be permitted to do so.»[1]

This fundamental consideration, which is another consequence of the exclusivity of the ICSID system, finds its expression in Article 27 of the ICSID Convention. That provision expressly prohibits a Contracting State from giving diplomatic protection, or bringing an international claim, in respect of a dispute which one of its nationals and

---

[1] Executive Directors' *Report, supra* note 3, para. 33.

another Contracting State have consented to submit to ICSID arbitration.[1]

The ICSID Convention's suspension of the right to exercise diplomatic protection need not, however, be seen purely from the viewpoint of the host country. For an investor, diplomatic protection by the home country is at best an uncertain remedy, and one that may often exacerbate rather than moderate a dispute. The ICSID system by contrast seeks to depoliticize the resolution of investment disputes in an effective and truly neutral forum, where the investor and the host State have equal opportunities and where disputes are to be settled according to objective non-political criteria.

III. The Role of the Multilateral Investment Guarantee Agency

A. Background

Despite the contributions of ICSID and other important instruments such as the International Finance Corporation, new mechanisms for encouraging a greater level of foreign direct investment are needed to reverse the negative trends prevailing at present. Commercial lending to developing countries has declined drastically, and official development assistance is stagnating. Foreign direct investment represents a source of external finance which holds great promise for substantial increases. However, direct investment flows to developing countries have not increased in recent years. On the contrary, the last few years have witnessed a sharp decline in such flows. There are strong indications that this decline can be explained in part by growing perceptions related to the non-commercial risks which face investors outside their home countries.

It is in this context that the initiative to create a globally operating investment guarantee agency under the World Bank's auspices was resumed by the World Bank's management in 1981.[2] As in the case of the ICSID Convention, extensive studies and consultations then took place, and support for the proposed new agency gradually broadened. From June to

[1] Under the ICSID Convention, diplomatic protection is suspended from the date of consent to ICSID arbitration (possibly subject to exhaustion of local remedies) until an award is rendered. It is only when the State party to the dispute, assuming that the award is rendered against it, fails to comply with the award, that the right of diplomatic protection is revived.

[2] See Address of World Bank President A.W. Clausen, 1981 Joint Annual Meetings of the World Bank and International Monetary Fund *Summary Proceedings* 15, 23. (1982).

September 1985, the Bank's Executive Directors met as a «Committee of the Whole» under the chairmanship of the Bank's Vice President and General Counsel in order to discuss a draft of the Convention Establishing the Multilateral Investment Guarantee Agency (the MIGA Convention). Assisted by experts from member governments and by a drafting team from the World Bank's Legal Department, the Committee of the Whole agreed on a text of the MIGA Convention on September 12, 1985, after twenty sessions of vivid and at times heated discussion.

After its formal approval by the World Bank's Executive Directors, the MIGA Convention was submitted to the Bank's Board of Governors for consideration at its Annual Meeting in October 1985 in Seoul. There the Governors adopted a resolution opening the MIGA Convention for signature by member governments of the World Bank and Switzerland.[1] Signatures of the Convention commenced forthwith (Ecuador, Korea and Turkey signed on October 11, 1985, the same date the Convention was opened for signature, and Senegal signed two weeks later).

The MIGA Convention will enter into force upon its ratification by five capital-exporting and fifteen capital-importing countries, provided that the total subscriptions of these countries amount to at least one-third of MIGA's authorized capital, or approximately $360 million.[2] It is expected that in the course of the coming twelve months the Convention may be signed by the number of countries whose ratification is required for its entry into force.

Five fundamental innovations distinguish MIGA from earlier schemes for a multilateral investment guarantee facility:

(i) While previous concepts focussed exclusively on guarantee operations, MIGA will provide a broader forum for international policy cooperation among capital-importing countries, capital-exporting countries and foreign investors. Insurance is only one means of achieving MIGA's broader objective of encouraging investment flows for productive purposes.

(ii) Earlier proposals focussed on investment flows from developed countries, but MIGA is directed also, and in fact specifically, to take part in the promotion of investment flows among developing countries.[3]

---

[1] The MIGA Convention, along with the Commentary thereon, will soon appear in *International Legal Materials* and, in early 1986, in the first issue of *ICSID Review – Foreign Investment Law Journal.*

[2] *MIGA Convention, Art. 61 (b).*

[3] *See MIGA Convention, Arts. 2 (b) and 23 (c).*

(iii) Unlike previous schemes, which envisaged an agency closely linked with the World Bank, MIGA is designed to be an autonomous institution which will operate on its own account and within its own responsibility while maintaining a symbolic, but significant linkage with the Bank. In accordance with Articles 32(b) and 33(b) of the MIGA Convention, the President of the Bank will be *ex officio* Chairman of the Agency's Board and in this capacity will nominate the person to be elected by the Board as MIGA's President.

(iv) Political oversight of and financial responsibility for MIGA will be shared by both home and host countries, with the latter eventually subscribing 40 percent of the capital and having one-half of the votes. By contrast, previous proposals envisaged an agency controlled and financed only by investors' home countries.

(v) More than in the previously conceived instruments, the MIGA Convention contains a number of safeguards which ensure the host governments' control over investment activities in their territories while requiring MIGA to work on the improvement of investment conditions and standards in agreement with these governments.

B. Operations

MIGA will aim to encourage the flow of investments for productive purposes among its member countries, and in particular to developing member countries.[1] Like ICSID, MIGA is intended to enhance mutual understanding and confidence between host governments and foreign investors. To fulfill its purposes, MIGA will guarantee eligible investments against losses resulting from non-commercial risk and carry out promotional activities.

Article 11 of the MIGA Convention specifically provides for coverage of four broad categories of non-commercial risk, but authorizes the Agency to cover any other non-commercial risk upon the joint application of the investor and the host country, provided the Agency's Board approves such coverage by a special majority decision. The four risks specified in the Convention are: (a) the transfer risk resulting from host government restrictions on currency conversion and transfer; (b) the risk of loss resulting from legislative actions or administrative actions or

[1] *Id.*, Art. 2.

omissions of the host government which have the effect of depriving the foreign investor of his ownership or control of, or substantial benefits from, his investment; (c) the repudiation or breach of government contracts in the cases where the investor has no access to a competent judicial or arbitral forum, or faces unreasonable delays in such a forum or is unable to enforce a judicial or arbitral decision issued in his favor; and (d) the risk of armed conflict and civil disturbance. At present, the «transfer risk» is probably the most relevant from the viewpoint of investors. Cases of outright expropriation have become infrequent, and we have seen that this is reflected in ICSID's experience.

The value of the expropriation coverage will depend largely on MIGA's ability to cope with the problem of «creeping expropriation» and expropriation in the guise of apparently legal measures adopted by the host government. Article 11(a)(ii) of the Convention excludes from coverage «non-discriminatory measures of general application which governments normally take for the purpose of regulating economic activity in their territories». This exclusion is not meant to confine coverage under that provision to outright expropriation. The exclusion applies only to host governmental measures that meet all its requirements, i.e. to measures that (a) do not discriminate against the investor, (b) are *normally* taken by governments, and (c) are taken for the purpose of regulating economic activities in the host country's territory. The Commentary on the Convention, which was also approved by the Bank's Executive Directors, lists as examples of such measures «taxation, environmental and labor legislation as well as normal measures for the maintenance of public safety». MIGA's regulations and the contracts of guarantee to be entered into between MIGA and the investors should define the risks to be covered precisely in order to avoid any misunderstanding in this respect. As the Convention states the above-mentioned exclusion in the context of the risks eligible for cover, such an exclusion should be made clear at the time of coverage and could not appropriately be cited as an excuse for non-payment by the Agency in respect of a loss resulting from a covered risk which is clearly described in a contract of guarantee signed by the Agency.

To be eligible, investments will have to be new, medium- or long-term, and must be judged by the Agency to be sound investments which contribute to the development of the host country.[1] While at the outset MIGA will focus on equity interests and other forms of direct investment, it may be authorized to expand coverage to «any other medium- or long-

[1] *Id.*, Art. 12.

term form of investment» under various forms of industrial cooperation such as management and service contracts, licensing and franchising agreements, turnkey contracts as well as arrangements concerning the transfer of technology and know-how where the investor assumes a stake in the performance of the venture.[1] This will enable MIGA to service several new types of investment, especially among developing member countries, which take non-equity forms.

Investors, to be eligible for the Agency's guarantee, must be nationals of a member country or, in the case of juridical persons (corporate investors), must either be incorporated and have their principal place of business in a member country, or the majority of their capital must be owned by nationals of a member or members.[2] In this context another innovative feature of the MIGA Convention should be noted: eligibility may, under certain conditions, be extended to nationals of the host country if they transfer the assets to be invested from abroad.[3] MIGA will therefore be able to assist member countries in their efforts to reverse capital flight.

In recognition of host governments' sovereign control over the admission of foreign investment into their territories and the treatment of such investment, Article 15 of the MIGA Convention provides that the Agency «shall not conclude any contract of guarantee before the host government has approved the issuance of the guarantee by the Agency against the risks designated for cover». The approval must hence extend both to MIGA's involvement, i.e., the issuance of a guarantee, and to the scope of MIGA's involvement, i.e., the risks designated for cover. A member government may, if it wishes, limit its use of MIGA's services to the coverage of investments by its nationals in foreign member countries without necessarily allowing it to cover foreign investments in its own territory. In short, MIGA's facilities, like those of ICSID, will only be made available where there is consent by all concerned.

In addition to its guarantee operations, MIGA will carry out a variety of promotional activities such as performing research, providing information on investment opportunities to foreign investors and policy advice to member governments, and such technical assistance as may be required in this field. Article 23(c) of the MIGA Convention provides that in its promotional efforts, MIGA «shall give particular attention ... to the importance of increasing the flow of investments among developing member countries».

---

[1] *Id.*
[2] *Id.*, Art. 13(a).
[3] *Id.*, Art. 13(c).

C. Organization, Membership and Voting

MIGA will have full juridical personality and will function autonomously. In particular, it will be both legally and financially separate from the World Bank. Like other international financial institutions, MIGA will have a Council of Governors composed of one representative of each member (and his alternate), a Board of Directors elected by the Council, and a chief executive officer selected by the Board and responsible for the ordinary business of the Agency.[1]

Membership in MIGA will be open to all members of the World Bank and to Switzerland on a voluntary basis.[2] As in the case of ICSID, every country will be free to join without any effect on its position in the World Bank or any other organization. I have mentioned that the MIGA Convention will enter into force upon its ratification by only twenty countries. This will give the Agency the opportunity to start operations at an early stage. It is hoped, however, that MIGA will gradually earn broad recognition and attract a large membership. It may be noted in this context that the ICSID Convention entered into force in 1966 upon its ratification by only twenty countries. That Convention, as I mentioned earlier, has now been ratified by eighty-seven States. MIGA's success both as an insurer and as a forum for the development of policies regarding foreign investment will depend on wide membership and support for its objectives.

The distribution of voting rights presents a further innovation which highlights the balance of interests maintained by the MIGA Convention. The management of the World Bank had originally proposed that voting power would be shared on an equal basis between home countries and host countries as groups, with countries initially classifying themselves as members of one of the two groups, subject to approval of the Agency's Council. During the discussions among the World Bank's Executive Directors, this proposal was challenged on the grounds that it cannot be foretold how many countries of either group will join MIGA from the outset and that in view of the unpredictable relative size of each of the two groups it is inequitable to allocate equal voting power to them before knowing the actual membership structure. However, the basic tenet of the management's proposal was generally accepted, namely that both groups should receive equal voting power when all members of the World Bank become members of MIGA.[3] In the first three years of its operations, the

---

[1] *Id.*, Art. 30.
[2] *Id.*, Art. 4(a).
[3] *Id.*, Art. 39(a) and Schedule A.

minority group would be guaranteed 40 percent of the total votes, through supplementary votes if required, and all decisions would be taken in this period by the special majority of two-thirds of the total votes representing not less than 55 percent of subscriptions in the Agency's capital.[1] The supplementary votes and the special majority requirement would be cancelled at the end of the three-year period. MIGA's Council will then review the voting structure with a view to reallocating shares to assure voting parity between both groups of countries once they subscribe in the reallocated shares.

D. Financing: Self-Sustenance and Joint Responsibility

MIGA is expected to meet its liabilities from premium income and other revenues such as return on its investments. Accordingly, Article 25 of the MIGA Convention directs the Agency to carry out its activities in accordance with sound business and prudent financial management practices. Under Article 26 of the Convention, MIGA will be able to vary its premiums in accordance with the actual risks assumed under its guarantees, but such variations will be based on the specifics of the investment and risks involved – and will not simply reflect a political judgment regarding the host country.

Directed to operate on a financially viable basis, MIGA, after it pays a claim, would assume the rights that the indemnified investor acquired against the host country as a result of the event giving rise to his claim. Such subrogation – a generally accepted principle of insurance law – will provide nothing more than the assignment of an existing claim from the investor to MIGA and will give MIGA no greater substantive rights than had been acquired by the investor.[2]

Disputes between MIGA and a host country with respect to such rights will normally by settled by negotiation. Failing negotiation, it is envisaged that either party to the dispute will have access to international arbitration unless both parties agree to resort first to conciliation.[3] However, MIGA will be authorized under the Convention to enter with individual host countries into bilateral agreements on the resolution of disputes according to alternative mechanisms, provided that the agreement is approved in each case by the Board by special majority prior to the undertaking by

[1] *Id.*, Arts. 3(d), 39(b) and 39(d).
[2] *Id.*, Art. 18.
[3] *Id.*, Art. 57 and Annex II.

the Agency of operations in the territory of the member concerned. Such agreements would supersede the dispute settlement mechanism provided in the MIGA Convention. Although the Convention directs the parties to use the mechanism provided for in its annex as a basis for their agreement,[1] it is obvious that such an agreement, if it is to be justified at all, would have to provide for different methods, which would presumably be satisfactory to the Agency and consistent with the constitutional requirements of the country concerned.

The principle of self-sustenance will be supported by arrangements to ensure the Agency's viability even when losses exceed reserves at a given moment. These arrangements include a combination of capital subscriptions and «sponsorship».

The Agency will initially have an authorized share capital of SDR 1 billion.[2] The shares will be subscribed by member countries in accordance with their relative economic strength as measured in the allocation of shares in the World Bank's capital. Only ten percent of the subscriptions will be paid in cash. An additional ten percent will be paid in the form of non-negotiable, non-interest-bearing promissory notes to be encashed only if needed by MIGA to meet its financial obligations.[3] The rest of the subscribed capital will be subject to call.[4] While developed member countries will make all payments in freely usable currencies, developing member countries will be able to make up to twenty-five percent of the paid-in cash portion of their subscriptions in their own currencies.[5] The amount of guarantees which MIGA may issue will initially not exceed one and one half times the amount of the subscribed capital plus reserves plus a portion of MIGA's reinsurance coverage (a 1.5:1 ratio).[6] Once MIGA accumulates a balanced risk portfolio and gains experience, it might increase this ratio up to a maximum of 5:1.[7]

In addition to the guarantee operations based on the Agency's capital and reserves, MIGA will be able to underwrite investments sponsored by member countries acting in fact as administrator of a separate sponsorship account. Revenues from sponsorship operations will be accumulated in a «Sponsorship Trust Fund» which will be kept apart from the Agency's own

---

[1] *Id.*, Art. 57(b).
[2] *Id.*, Art. 5(a).
[3] *Id.*, Art. 7(i).
[4] *Id.*, Art. 7(ii).
[5] *Id.*, Art. 8(a).
[6] *Id.*, Art. 22(a).
[7] *Id.*

accounts. Claims and other expenses resulting from sponsorship operations will be paid out of this fund. Upon its depletion, remaining liabilities will be shared by sponsoring countries only, each in the proportion which the guarantees sponsored by it bear to the total guarantees sponsored by all sponsoring countries. This «sponsorship window» represents a particularly interesting feature of MIGA, not only because it has no financial ceiling but also because it allows coverage of investments in all countries and not just in MIGA's developing member countries.

The combination of capital subscription and sponsorship is another factor which distinguishes MIGA from the international investment insurance schemes previously discussed in the World Bank. These schemes relied chiefly on sponsorship by investors' home countries (with some suggesting an initial contribution from the World Bank). Yet, adoption of this concept would have made the Agency dependent to a great extent on one group of members. By contrast, MIGA will primarily rely on capital subscriptions from all member countries and will have the necessary independence to carry out its development mandate in the common interest of all its members.

E. MIGA as an Instrument for the Improvement of Investment Conditions

MIGA has a mandate to seek to stabilize and improve investment climates in its developing member countries and thus stimulate investment flows to these countries. This mandate is reflected in a number of the provisions of the Convention.[1] It is reinforced by MIGA's institutional structure and internal dynamics.

In the past, the need for fair and stable investment conditions has been emphasized from the perspective of investors and their home countries. However, host countries clearly serve their national interests by pro-

---

[1] The Preamble recognizes that investment flows to developing countries «would be facilitated and further encouraged by alleviating concerns related to non-commercial risks» and expresses the desire of the Contracting States to enhance investment flows «on the basis of fair and stable standards for the treatment of foreign investment». Article 12(d)(iv) makes satisfactory investment conditions in the host country, «including the availability of fair and equitable treatment and legal protection for the investment» pre-requisites for coverage; and Article 23 provides that MIGA will «seek to remove impediments . . . to the flow of investment to developing member countries», «encourage the amicable settlement of investment disputes between investors and host countries», endeavor to conclude with developing member countries agreements on the treatment of guaranteed investments, and «promote and facilitate . . . agreements . . . on the promotion and protection of investments».

viding sound investment conditions. Their ability to attract badly needed resources and to bargain for better terms and conditions is obviously strengthened by the availability of better investment climates in their territories. The establishment of an international development institution, financed and controlled jointly by developed and developing countries, manifests the common interest in creating a favorable investment climate in the latter countries.

Frequently, issues related to foreign investment have become intermingled with the political interests of home and host countries. As a result, investment disputes often became highly politicized. Like ICSID, MIGA seeks to remove these disputes from the political arena. MIGA will endeavor to ensure that such disputes will be resolved only on the basis of legal and economic criteria.[1] It is explicitly prohibited from interfering in the political affairs of its members.[2] Moreover, MIGA's internal dynamics will result in its playing an important role as an intermediary between investors and host countries. To attract business and generate revenues, it must offer effective guarantee protection and pay claims which are justified. To minimize underwriting losses, it must avoid claims and, where they do occur, secure recovery from the host country whenever possible. Recovery procedures could jeopardize MIGA's good relations with developing member countries which could easily curtail MIGA's operations by denying their approval for further guarantees. Therefore MIGA must ensure that the goodwill of member countries is not lost and that their common interest in the Agency's functioning prevails over the conflicting interests in a particular dispute.

The competing pressures will force MIGA to cover risks that are unlikely to invite adverse host governmental action which could give rise to claims. At the same time, MIGA will have to ensure that these investments are accorded stable and predictable treatment. Article 12(d) of the MIGA Convention reflects this balanced approach by directing MIGA to restrict its coverage to investments which are compatible with the host country's laws and declared development objectives and to require, on the other hand, that these investments be given adequate treatment and protection.

---

[1] Cf., Meron, «The World Bank and Insurance,» 47 *Brit. Y.B. Int'l L.* 301, 312 (1974-1975): «. . . the very raison d'être of the establishment of a multilateral insurance agency was to make subrogation into a non-political, technical, non-confrontation issue»; Martin, «Multilateral Investment Insurance: the OECD Proposal,» 8 *Harv. Int'l L.J.* 280, 318-319 (1967): «With an international agency it is more likely that the claim will be treated as the legal issue that it should be.» Both comments were made in respect of earlier proposals regarding the establishment of a multilateral agency for political risk insurance.

[2] MIGA Convention, Art. 34.

Where disputes nevertheless arise between investors and host countries, MIGA's involvement, like that of ICSID, will increase the prospects for amicable settlements. The MIGA Convention indeed directs MIGA to encourage such settlements.[1] In case of disputes, MIGA's assessment, based on the broad information available to it, together with its worldwide experience, is likely to moderate the conflicting claims of an investor and a host country and promote a settlement.

Another way in which MIGA may encourage host governments and investors to arrive at amicable settlements is to reduce the financial burden of any settlements by accepting the local currency of the host country on a temporary basis and paying the investor out of its own funds in freely usable currency. MIGA might then, under an agreement with the host country,[2] sell the local currency to the World Bank, other international institutions, companies importing goods from the host country, or to the host government itself over a period of time and restore its financial position accordingly. MIGA might also facilitate the settlement by paying the investor in cash and accepting debt instruments from the government as reimbursement. As a variant of this approach, MIGA could persuade the investor to accept installments rather than insisting on a cash payment by backing the government's commitments with its guarantee. In view of its developmental mandate and policy interests, MIGA can be anticipated to facilitate settlements amicably at least as successfully as some of the national agencies have done.[3]

---

[1] Id., Art. 23(b)(i).

[2] Article 18(c) of the MIGA Convention directs MIGA to «seek to enter into agreements with host countries on ... uses of ... currencies to the extent that they are not freely usable».

[3] The US Overseas Private Investment Corporation (OPIC) has been especially successful. According to unpublished figures recently obtained from OPIC, that Corporation has settled claims in the total amount of $96 million by paying compensation in cash to the investor while accepting installments from the host government; and claims totalling some $292 million, by persuading investors to accept host government commitments backed by OPIC guarantees or by a combination of cash payment and guarantees.

IV. Conclusion

In the framework of a system that is voluntary and flexible, ICSID affords uniquely effective legal protection to foreign private investment. One of MIGA's principal tasks will be to provide foreign private investors with guarantee protection against non-commercial risks. But I hope that I have demonstrated that the roles of MIGA and ICSID are broader than this. The two agencies are above all designed to promote an atmosphere of mutual confidence between foreign investors and their host countries conducive to a larger flow of private international capital into those countries which wish to attract it. Such an atmosphere of mutual confidence could prove to be ultimately the best protection for foreign private investment.

Aussenwirtschaft, 41. Jahrgang (1986), Heft I, Grüsch: Rüegger, S.123–133

Coverage of Political Risk by National Insurance Agencies: The German Investment Guarantee Scheme

Dr. Jörg-Dietrich Wurmstich
Director, Treuarbeit Aktiengesellschaft, Hamburg

The Basic Ideas of the Scheme

The Investment Guarantee Scheme of the Federal Republic of Germany was created in 1958 and 1959 and became effective at the beginning of 1960. It was the third scheme of this kind in the world, after the US-American scheme and the Japanese scheme. The reason for the relatively early installation of the German scheme was that German firms were more reluctant with regard to foreign investments than firms in other countries: within 30 years they had lost twice nearly all their foreign investments during and after the two World Wars.

The scheme was created to reassure potential investors afraid of losing their money invested abroad through political risks such as the risk of expropriation, war risk, and the transfer risk connected with the retransfer of capital and the transfer of interest and profits. The Investment Guarantee Scheme was meant to facilitate the decision of German investors to invest abroad.

The legal authorization does not expressly limit these guarantees to investments in developing countries. Also the US-American guarantees, in the beginning, were issued for investments in industrialized countries, especially in Europe. Thus, they contributed to the reconstruction of Europe after the war, as the ERP- (European Relief Programme) funds granted by the United States did. However, from the beginning the German guarantees have only been issued for investments in developing countries as the pertaining regulations deem investments especially worthy of promotion when they strengthen relations between Germany and developing countries.

As German Investment Guarantees are meant to allay investors' fears of losing their capital invested in the foreign enterprise, coverage is limited to the amount which flows from the German enterprise into the foreign enterprise. A later increase in value of the investment will not come under the coverage in principle.

There is also another limit for indemnification. If the foreign enterprise suffers losses due to commercial risks before it is affected by political risks the losses due to commercial reasons shall not be indemnified together with the losses due to political reasons. Consequently the amount of loss to be taken into account for an indemnification is limited to the actual value of the foreign enterprise or the German share in it just before the political event occurred.

These are the basic ideas of the German Investment Guarantee Scheme.

The Financial and Organizational Structure of the Scheme

The German Investment Guarantee Scheme is financially based on the budget of the Federal Republic of Germany, meaning that all expenditures as payments of indemnifications to investors are paid out of the Federal budget and all revenues as premiums flow into the budget. So these guarantees are backed by the full financial power of the state. This might be deemed to be of importance, as the political risks in quite different countries all over the world as covered by the investment guarantees do not appear to be calculable – contrary to those risks covered traditionally by the commercial insurance business –, at least not for periods of 15 or 20 years for which these guarantees are written without the guarantor's right to give notice. Also the other existing 19 national schemes for investment guarantees are based on the financial power of a state, the issuing agency either being a governmental institution as e.g. a ministry or – when the agency is a private firm – being backed financially by the state, e.g. by reguarantees.

The decisions whether to issue a guarantee are made by an Interministerial Committee. In this committee the Ministry of Economics, the Ministry of Finance, the Ministry of Foreign Affairs, and the Ministry of Economic Co-Operation (colloquially the «Ministry for Development Aid») are represented with voting power. Additionally, without voting power, there are representatives from industry, trade and banking as experts. A consortium has been commissioned to manage the German investment guarantees. This consortium has been formed by the Hermes Kreditversicherungs-Aktiengesellschaft (Credit Insurance Company) and by the Treuarbeit Aktiengesellschaft, Wirtschaftsprüfungsgesellschaft, Steuerberatungsgesellschaft (chartered accountants, tax advisers and trustees company), the latter being the leading company.

Eligibility for Guarantee

In order to be eligible an investor has to have his seat or domicile in the Federal Republic of Germany including West Berlin. It is not a prerequisite for eligibility that the majority of shares in an investing company are held by German nationals. However, if the majority of shares are held by nationals of another state or if the investor is controlled by nationals of another state the guarantee does not cover the risks originating from the relation between this other state and the host country. In cases in which an investment is made via a German affiliate of a foreign industrial group for the sole reason of obtaining a German investment guarantee the application for a guarantee will be turned down. In order to be eligible the investment has to be related to the objectives and the business of the German investor.

The investment to be guaranteed has to be worthy of promotion and should preferably strengthen relations between the Federal Republic of Germany and developing countries. It is an essential of the worthiness of promotion that the capital to be invested is accompanied by entrepreneurial activities of the German investor in the host country, such as e.g. the contribution of technical know-how or management. Purely financial investments for making profits are not eligible.

In principal investments in all lines of business are eligible, provided they are open for foreign investment according to the laws of the host country.

One of the prerequisites for a guarantee is that there is sufficient legal protection for the investment in the host country. This legal protection may be granted either by an Investment Protection Treaty[1] or, as long as an Investment Protection Treaty has not yet been concluded, by the constitution and the national laws of the host country. Besides, the question of legal protection and a good investment climate is of importance not only for the decision of the Interministerial Committee whether to issue a guarantee but also for the investor. A potential investor may ask whether an

---

[1]see Burkhardt Hans-Martin, Investment Protection Treaties: Recent Trends and Prospects, in this volume.

investment protection treaty has been concluded with the host country he has in mind and whether this host country is eligible for guarantee. If both answers are affirmative sometimes investors do not think it necessary to take out a guarantee for their investments. Additionally, in some cases claims for the payment of an indemnification under the guarantee have been averted by reminding the government of the host country that its action affecting the investment was not in accordance with the Investment Protection Treaty.

Investments to be guaranteed may be made in the form of equity participation, investment-like loans or so-called endowment capital.

Both equity participations in companies limited by shares and in partnerships are eligible. Also a share-holding of 100 per cent in the foreign enterprise is eligible, provided that such a participation is permitted according to the laws of the host country. A country in Africa, e.g., has stipulated maximum percentages for foreign participation for many lines of business; in some lines of business no foreign participation is permitted. In Latin American countries foreign majority is partly not permitted or needs approval by the government.

The eligibility of investment-like loans had to be included as often the necessary capital for a firm is not completely provided for in the form of share capital but partly also in the form of shareholders' loans. For guarantee purposes a loan will be looked upon as investment-like when the lender already has an equity participation in the foreign enterprise or is going to acquire such a participation. Additionally, the term of the loans has to be at least five years and the loan should have a moderate rate of interest.

Endowment capital is capital provided for an overseas branch or establishment not being a legal entity of its own.

Also earnings, as e.g. dividends or claims for the payment of interest, may be included in the guarantee. However, this earnings cover does not mean that the guarantee becomes operative if the foreign enterprise does not make profits and cannot pay dividends due to political risks. Only if already existing claims for the payment of distributed dividends or due interest cannot be fulfilled due to political risks does the guarantee become operative. In practice only cases have come up in which the payment of dividends or interest could not be effected due to the lack of foreign currency of the host country. The earnings cover is limited to 8 per cent p.a. and to 24 per cent of the invested capital over the term of the guarantee.

Finally, it should be emphasized that only new investments are eligible, meaning that the investment is made after an application for a guarantee has been filed. As the guarantees are meant as an incentive for additional investments, such cases have had to be excluded from eligibility in which the investor made his investment some time ago without a guarantee but now wishes to have his investment insured against political risks.

The Political Risks Covered by the Guarantee

The risks covered by the guarantee are: the risk of expropriation, war risk, and transfer risk.

Expropriation is defined as follows: nationalization, confiscation, expropriation, or acts or the illegal failure to act on the part of the government or other authorities, which have an effect equivalent to confiscation/ expropriation. This wording does not only comprise formal explicit expropriation. Nowadays the risk of expropriation becomes apparent in other forms. In one African country, e.g., individual maximum percentages for foreign investments in the individual lines of business were stipulated. Consequently quite a number of investors had to reduce the percentage of their share participation in the foreign enterprises. The shares had to be sold to nationals of this country.

The price of the shares had to be approved by the authorities. Given this situation, selling prices were mostly below the actual value of the share-participation which had to be sold. Another example is the replacement of the directors elected by the shareholders by so-called inspectors commissioned by the foreign state, who took over the management and prevented the shareholders from executing any rights related to their shares. Also so-called creeping or sneaking expropriation has to be mentioned. This is a number of acts by the authorities, whereby each individual act taken separately cannot be deemed to be expropriation, but where all acts together have the effect of an expropriation. In principle, acts of the state to control the economy (as they were taken also in European countries especially in the years after the last World War and still exist in some fields as, e.g., price control) do not come under the covered risk. However, if such acts are exclusively aimed at all foreigners or at an individual foreign enterprise, the situation may be judged upon otherwise.

War risk does not only comprise wars between states, but also other armed conflicts, revolutions and rebellions; not, however, civil unrest of a lesser degree.

Transfer risk may become apparent as so-called active blockage of transfer or as so-called passive blockage. Both normally are due to a lack of foreign currency in the host country. However, the former is based on a law or decree of the host country prohibiting its nationals from paying foreign debts or on a unilateral moratorium by the host country, whereas the latter means a failure to effect transfer and conversion by the Central Bank simply due to a lack of foreign currency.

Due to the foreign debt crises of many developing countries transfer risk has an increased importance nowadays. Nevertheless, the consequences of transfer risk for investments are often of a somewhat lesser degree than they are in the field of export credit guarantees. An exporter expects payment for the goods he has exported under all circumstances. However, as a rule, amounts invested in equity participation are destined to stay in the host country forever. Also the principal of a part of the investment-like loans is not going to be re-transferred but will be transformed into share capital after some years. With regard to earnings it should be mentioned that, especially in developing countries, it takes some time until the new enterprise becomes profitable and then again a part of these profits is not transferred home but used for the expansion of the foreign enterprise. Due to these facts the amounts to be transferred in the field of investment guarantees are relatively lower compared with the insured amount than in the field of export credit guarantees.

Total Losses and Partial Losses

With regard to cover for total losses and partial losses the following may be pointed out: If the political risks affect the relationship between the investor and the foreign enterprise, e.g., if the investor is expropriated of half of his shares in the foreign enterprise, also partial losses of the investment will be indemnified. However, if the foreign enterprise is deprived of its assets or its assets are destroyed, only total losses will be indemnified. That means an indemnification will only be paid if either all the assets have been taken or destroyed or if such an essential part of the assets have been taken or destroyed that the foreign enterprise cannot in the long run be operated without loss and, consequently, the investment must be considered lost.

The Amount of Indemnification

As far as the amount is concerned which the guarantor has to pay as indemnification for the loss of an investment, the following should be kept in mind: The guarantee is to safeguard the investor from losing the amount (either in money or the value of contributions in kind such as machinery) he has transferred from his enterprise to the foreign enterprise. Consequently the indemnification is limited to the amount of the value of the investor's contribution to the foreign enterprise (contribution value). Later increases in the value of the investor's shares in the enterprise, e.g., due to retained earnings in the foreign enterprise (unless they are formally converted into nominal share capital) are not covered. If the investor's contribution consists of money transferred to the foreign enterprise it is not difficult, as a rule, to assess the contribution value. If the contribution is made in kind, e.g., if the investor contributes machinery to the foreign enterprise in consideration of the share subscribed by him, the contribution value is equal to the costs of acquisition or the costs of manufacturing the machinery, or the original costs as they are also called, plus the costs for the transport of the machinery to the foreign enterprise. If the machinery has already been used in the investor's factory the contribution value, as a rule, is equal to the amount at which this machinery is shown in the investor's balance sheet, taking into account generally accepted principals of accounting, but without making special depriciations as admitted under tax laws.

Some difficulties may arise if the investor contributes patents and know-how which have not been bought but have come into existence in the investor's own firm. Under German law such items may not be entered in the balance sheet. Additionally it is often very difficult or impossible to determine the cost attributable to such items. In some rare and special cases the contribution value of such items has been fixed in co-operation with the investor, taking into account such thoughts as a capitalization of royalties for such items in comparable markets. If the foreign enterprise is a joint venture between the investor and a strong national partner in the host country the agreement between the two partners on the price for these items may be taken as some circumstantial evidence for the reasonable price of these items.

As already mentioned, there is one exception to the principle that later increases in the value of the investment will not increase the insured amount. If the investor receives bonus shares originating from profits out of the guaranteed investment having been put aside as available reserves and now being formally transformed into share capital, the contribution value and the insured amount will be increased accordingly. Although there is no additional flow of capital from the investor's enterprise to the foreign enterprise, it has to be taken into account that it would have been possible – at least theoretically – for these profits to have been distributed as dividends to the investor, who then could have used this amount for subscribing additional shares. In the latter case the newly subscribed shares would be eligible as new investment. It was not deemed reasonable to cause the investor to take this indirect way to achieve eligibility, as this indirect way is often connected with higher cost and taxes and may not be approved by other partners in the investment.

Another limit for indemnification is the actual value of the investment just before it is affected by one of the covered political risks. It may be understandable that the state as guarantor does not want to indemnify the investor for commercial losses which appeared before the political events affected the investment. However, sometimes diverging considerations are necessary. If the foreign enterprise is still under construction when it is struck by a political event and when there are no profits but only losses in the pre-completion period, whether carried on the assets side of the balance sheet or not, one has to judge whether it would have been possible for the enterprise to have made good these losses without the political event. If the investor in question had already founded affiliates in many countries, all working very successfully, one can assume that also this affiliate would have worked successfully without political interference. Consequently indemnification has to be based on the full contribution value.

The actual value of the investment is determined as a value in Deutsche Mark attributable to the investment at the date immediately before damage, taking into consideration valuation principles from the field of economics and being based on the annual balance sheets and profit and loss accounts furnished by the investor up to this date. Taking into account the mentioned principles of valuation it is possible also to consider, e.g., hidden reserves originating from inflation.

Other national guarantee schemes partly base the computation of indemnification on the book value of the investment as shown in the balance sheet of the foreign enterprise, this balance sheet having been made up according to generally accepted principles of accounting in the guarantor's country. This book value is converted into the currency of the guarantor's country at the present exchange rate. In host countries with a high inflation rate this may lead to the result that the calculated loss arrived at is much too low expressed in the currency of the guarantor's country. For this reason some of these national schemes do not base their calculation any longer on the historic cost of acquisition of the assets of the foreign enterprise but on present replacement cost.

It may be mentioned that the investor has to participate in every covered loss (self-participation or co-insurance). As a rule, and as a minimum, self-participation is fixed at 5 per cent.

Premiums

When an investor considers taking out a guarantee for his investment the cost of this guarantee is of importance to him. As the German guarantee scheme does not work on a capital basis but indemnifications under the guarantees are paid out of the budget, it was not deemed necessary to set aside reserves or provisions according to the rules of commercial insurance business. Otherwise considerable provisions would have had to be made, due to the incalculability of political risks over a very long period. When forming the provision it would also have been necessary to take into account that the extent of damages fluctuates enormously from year to year. However, as these guarantees are financially borne by the state, after some years of experience the premium could be fixed at 0.5 per cent p.a. on the actual insured amount. Up to now this low premium has been sufficient to keep the system self-supporting. However, it has to be admitted that fundamental political evolutions or revolutions in some countries might affect this negatively.

The Development of the Scheme

The first guárantees were issued in January 1960. Already in 1959 17 applications amounting to DM 82 million had been filed. In 1960 another 65 applications were filed amounting to DM 142 million. By the end of the year 1984 3,710 applications amounting to DM 13,056 million had been filed; this means an average of about 150 applications and ½ billion DM per year. Of these filed applications 2,327 applications amounting to DM 7,171 million have been accepted for cover. The total of insured amounts of all guarantees outstanding at the end of 1984 was about

DM 5 billion. These outstanding guarantees are related to the following regions: Europe, including Turkey, about 10 per cent, Asia 15 per cent, Africa 41 per cent, Latin America 31 per cent. The indemnifications paid under the guarantees amount to nearly DM 20 million half of which has been recovered in the meantime.

Private Insurance Industry and National Guarantee Schemes

As mentioned before, it seems to be impossible to calculate in a reasonable way those political risks as they are covered by the national schemes over a period of 15 or 20 years. This explains why it was the states which first entered this new field of insurance in view of their politically motivated intention to promote investments in developing countries. The first offers of the private insurance industry – many years ago – to cover investments against political risks had a very short term, high premiums and a very limited extent of cover. In the meantime the private insurance industry has experience of insurance of investments against political risks and they nowadays can present much more interesting offers. There are cases in which investors having guarantees under the German national scheme have also concluded insurance contracts with the private insurance industry. They have taken out private insurance for those investments which cannot be covered by the national scheme as e.g. old investments or such investments for which the maximum term of 20 years for the guarantee has expired. Here it became apparent that it may be very useful to discuss how to adapt the terms and conditions of the private insurance to those of the national agency (the terms of the national agency are mostly ruled by laws and regulations and cannot be altered so easily). This is especially true when different participations (e.g., new ones and old ones) in the same foreign enterprise are to be insured partly with the private insurance industry and partly with the national scheme. It should be made quite clear which of the two covers an individual share, especially with regard to different bonus shares, etc. issued over time. Also, if an investor intends to insure an increase in value of his investment with the private insurance industry (the underlying profits not having been formally transferred into share capital and therefore not insurable under the national scheme) the investor has to be told that in such a case the indemnification paid by the private insurance industry has to be deducted from his loss when calculating the indemnification under the guarantee by the national scheme, thus decreasing the indemnification to be paid by the national scheme. It should also be mentioned that the terms and conditions of the private investment insurance industry on one hand and those of the national scheme on the other partly stipulate contradictory obligations for the investor which he cannot fulfil simultaneously. Therefore talks between the investor, representatives of the private insurance industry and of the national agency may be recommended in such cases.

Aussenwirtschaft, 41. Jahrgang (1986), Heft I, Grüsch: Rüegger, S.135–139

Coverage of Political Risk by the Private Insurance Industry

Julian G. Y. Radcliffe
Director, Hogg Robinson Group p.l.c., London

The foundation of political risk insurance at Lloyds and indeed with American insurers, came from their insurance of marine interests. Virtually every ship, aircraft and cargo in the world is insured for political risks. Ships going up the Gulf at the moment to pick up oil often are paying premiums that equate to 10% of their hull values. So this is a business which has a fair degree of risk. In the early 1970s, we decided that there was a niche we could fill providing insurance for multinational companies for their overseas investments and exports when they could not get the cover they required from their government schemes. We do not see ourselves as competitive with the government schemes, and indeed we frequently advise a company to go to a government scheme and often will only consider them if they have been turned down. There are occasions where we are competitive, but on the whole we try to be a complementary alternative and to fit in with the government schemes, because we recognize their strengths – they can provide a long-term guarantee which we cannot. The maximum period for which we will usually insure an investment is 3 to 5 years, and although we can roll that forward so that the investor has always that period in front of him, I appreciate that this is a weakness. I fear that it will take some time before we are able to give guarantees for a 15 year period, and the reason for that is that we do not believe it commercially sound practice for us to lock ourselves into a fixed premium when we cannot predict what the loss experience will be.

I believe that we have a sufficient record of not increasing premiums extortionately that most investors will feel – given a period of time to test us – that we are not unreasonable when the claim can be seen coming. We do not increase the premiums to say 50% p.a.

Secondly we cannot provide war-coverage. We are working towards extending the coverage we can give today, which is for riots and strikes and civil commotion and terrorism. We are looking to extend that to include war risks, but I do not believe that we shall ever give cover for wars involving two of the major five powers, or a war involving a nuclear explosion. I believe that it would be irresponsible for us to do so, even if everybody will have bigger problems than their overseas investments on that day.

Thirdly we cannot provide in many countries the same degree of inconvertability cover as the government scheme can. In certain cases as in the USA, the Overseas Private Investment Corporation (O.P.I.C.) can use blocked dollars for running American embassies. We do not have the same requirement for the use of blocked currency and therefore we have been sometimes unable to give the same cover as the government schemes have.

So those are our weaknesses. What are our strengths? Dr. Wurmstich mentioned some: We can insure existing investments as well as new. We are very flexible about how we structure the policy, so for example we might say to a company that we will insure any losses they have in excess of 20 million dollars in a year. So the company then knows that it will never have to go to its shareholders with a real tale of disaster because we are giving cover of $200 million in excess of $20 million. They can self insure the 20 and this is a way of reducing the premiums. We can insure loss of profits and business interruption risks. For example, if you put an investment into a country to obtain raw material, you are not really interested in what happens to the capital, you are interested in whether you get the oil or the copper or the agriculture produce. And we therefore tailor the policy to reflect the loss if you never get the tomatoes or whatever it is which you need for the factory. We can also insure 10% of a risk or 90% and we do not mind which we do. We can insure any nationality and indeed we have insured over 40 different nationalities of ownership in 120 countries in 70 types of industry.

As for the assessment of our premium rates, they are infinitely variable from 0.001% to 20%. It is certainly to some degree by guess that we find the premium rate. But also the premium rates are not really a reflection of the true actuarial or some theoretical analysis of the risk; they are a reflection of the law of supply and demand. So, if a company comes in and wishes to insure in Saudi-Arabia and we are already heavily involved in Saudi-Arabia, then the premium rate goes up and likewise we use the premium rates to arrive at a balanced portfolio. We are constantly seeking to insure investments in countries where we are not overexposed, to insure different nationalities of investors which we consider as important as the location of the investment, and to perhaps insure types of industry which we have not hitherto covered.

The values insured when this market started in 1972 was about eight million dollars maximum, but recently policies have been done for 500 million dollars! So the market has gone from eight to 500 in 12 years. The market has reduced in capacity a little recently, due to contractions in the general insurance business and losses on political risks and in other classes. But after a year or two of consolidation, I expect that there will be a significant increase in the volume of business we do. Nobody knows the exact figures because we do not centralize them, but I expect that we are talking about permanent investment premiums to the private market of 40 or 50 million dollars at least. But at a 1% premium, obviously we must be talking of investment insured in excess of 3 billion.

Now let us consider claims, because there is no point in insuring unless someone eventually picks up a claim. We have paid claims in 28 countries and they have varied from a German investor on an island who had his plantation confiscated, to a company which had a soap factory in Africa confiscated, to construction companies in Iran, to one Arab investor in another Arab country where an investment was deemed to be expropriated. Indeed the variants are almost infinite and many of these have been creeping expropriation claims as well as some which have been clear outright confiscations of 100%.

We have recently developed a number of adjunct services which lie alongside the political risk market. Initially you start off with a financial indemnity and then very often the fire underwriter becomes as important in terms of providing sprinkler engineering as he does in terms of providing fire insurance and so that has happened with political risks. We are increasingly providing advice on political risk management; we often have to do a study for a company which is unable to pass on the premiums for investment insurance and therefore has to weigh the premiums against the probability of loss. We run a lot of training schemes on political risk management for multinational corporations and banks and for people working in government export credit schemes and we also are improving our ability to help on recoveries.

We are handling with a small team some of the British ECGD losses in Iran and we are handling claims for some other governments as well. Some recoveries can be done through the Paris Club and by government to government negotiation. But for other cases which might involve a private buyer or a single investment, it may be difficult for a government to get involved and they may wish to use a third party. It may also be an uninsured investment in which case we could be retained and undertake the fact finding and hopefully the eventual conclusion in order to recover sums owed to underwriters and thereby maintain a stable underwriting market. Lloyds and other insurers will in the long term be considered very important in developing expertise on this sort of problems. Lloyds itself has a somewhat supra-national organisation or position which allows us to go on operating in virtually any country of the world whatever the chaos may be.

One of the reasons why this market has not grown as fast as I think it could do and perhaps should do is because of the reluctance of the bankers to accept private market insurance policies as being sufficient for them to take political risks off their sovereign country limits or, at least, to pay some attention in looking at their aggregate limits on a country as to whether something is insured in the private market or not. Some banks, including the Scandinavian banks, are using the private market very aggressively. Some American banks are doing the same. Some French too, but German and Swiss banks and some British banks have been much more reluctant and I think that may be to their disadvantage, although I would certainly not encourage them to rush in where angels should fear to tread in terms of extending credits to the developing countries. But I would also like to say that the private insurance market is often competing with some banks because the banks are the biggest providers of political risk insurance, not that they recognize that. Whereas a political risk insurer is charging a one percent premium, is looking to spread his portfolio, is backed up by a reinsurance and indeed has an accounting system designed to pay out claims, the bankers have been accepting political risks at one sixteenth of one percent without any reinsurance, without a balanced portfolio and with no ability to pay claims or at least to recognize claims in their accounting. That is one of the reasons why I have been giving some help to the Institute of International Finance as to how it is that banks can continue to develop their lending to the Third World using some of the principals of insurance which hitherto they have somewhat neglected.

Perhaps I could just emphasize some of the things the private market has done and is doing which may be of interest as indicators of our role in the future. During the Suez Canal blockade when there were many ships in the Canal owned by underwriters, Lloyds actually had representatives of the Egyptian and Israeli government together with the Dutch Salvage companies negotiating for the opening of the Suez Canal. I do believe that there is a very important role which the private market can provide in terms of recovery negotiations when other avenues may have failed, and indeed we consider that an important part of maintaining a stable market as well as providing a service to multinational companies who may not even be insured. And I think I am right in saying that the multinational companies do not insure all their investments against political risks and yet they all insure to a greater or lesser extent their assets against fire and their products against liabilities. Political risks in the worst case can be a more catastrophic hazard because there is no question of reselling or rebuilding in the country from which you are evicted and in some ways it represents a failure by us that we have not managed to produce a product which is really acceptable to those companies, as well as perhaps a failure by the companies to recognize some of risks that they are running.

Autoren

Alejo, F. Javier
International Finance Corporation, 1818 H Street, N.W., Washington, D.C. 20433, USA

Amstutz, Max D.
Dr., «Holderbank» Financières Glarus AG, CH-1298 Céligny

Bergsten, C. Fred
Dr., Institute for International Economics, 11 Dupont Circle, N.W., Washington, D.C. 20036, USA

Burkhardt, Hans-Martin
Dr., Bundesministerium für Wirtschaft, Postfach 14 02 60, D-5300 Bonn 1

Hauser, Heinz
Prof. Dr., Schweizerisches Institut für Aussenwirtschafts-, Struktur- und Regionalforschung, Dufourstrasse 48, CH-9000 St.Gallen

Hegewisch, Adolfo
Ministry of Control of Foreign Investment, Mexico

Huber, Klaus
Dr., Schweizerische Bankgesellschaft, Bahnhofstrasse 45, CH-8021 Zürich

Maucher, Helmut
Nestlé S.A., CH-1800 Vevey

Pollan, Hans
Dr., International Finance Corporation, New Zealand House, 15th Floor, Haymarket, London, SW1 4TE, England

Radcliffe, Julian G.Y.
Hogg Robinson Group p.l.c., 1, Portsoken Street, London, E1 8DF, England

Shihata, Ibrahim F.I.
Dr., The World Bank, 1818 H Street, N.W., Washington, D.C. 20433, USA

Sommaruga, Cornelio
Dr., Bundesamt für Aussenwirtschaft, Bundeshaus Ost, CH-3003 Bern

Wurmstich, Jörg-Dietrich
Dr., Treuarbeit Aktiengesellschaft, New York Ring 13, D-2000 Hamburg 60